OCCASIONAL PAPER 17

PRIVATE RENTED HOUSING IN THE 1980s AND 1990s

CHRISTINE M. E. WHITEHEAD
AND MARK P. KLEINMAN

Department of Land Economy
University of Cambridge

GRANTA EDITIONS

Published by Granta Editions Ltd, 47 Norfolk St, Cambridge
© C. M. E. Whitehead and M. P. Kleinman

ISBN: 0 906782 23 6

313642

Production services by Book Production Consultants,
47 Norfolk St, Cambridge
Printed by Paradigm Print, The Chaucer Press, Bungay, Suffolk

Typeset by Witwell Ltd, Liverpool

Cover Design by Averne

FOREWORD

The Department of Land Economy, which was established in 1961 in the University of Cambridge, is concerned with the study of the use, management and development of land, the built environment and other natural resources. The subject involves analysis of patterns of land use, both urban and rural and of the dynamics of land use change within different types of institutional and legislative frameworks and within countries at different levels of economic development. Of special concern to the Department are the processes whereby individuals, private companies and public agencies resolve conflicts over the use and development of land, the built environment and other natural resources.

Land economy is an interdisciplinary subject which draws particularly upon concepts and analysis developed within economics, law and political science. A deliberate interdisciplinary use of key concepts and analysis affords distinctive insights into the determinants of past, present and future land use patterns, land development and public policy.

This Occasional Paper series represents the findings of some of the research undertaken within the Department. It is, however, a series open to the work of others outside the University of Cambridge. Published with financial assistance from the Development Fund of the Department of Land Economy, its sole objective is to provide succinct and readable analyses of interest to the specialist and to the general public.

Cambridge   G. C. Cameron
Michaelmas Term 1986   Professor of Land Economy

OCCASIONAL PAPERS obtainable by post, (prices on request)
from:

Department of Land Economy, University of Cambridge,
19 Silver Street, Cambridge CB3 9EP.

1. Measurement of Urban Land Use
   R. C. FORDHAM, 1974

2. Mobility of Farm Workers
   RUTH GASSON, 1974

3. Land Reform in Ireland
   C. F. KOLBERT and T. O'BRIEN, 1975

4. Provision of Tied Cottages
   RUTH GASSON, 1975

5. Beef Cattle and Sheep 1910–40.
   EDITH H. WHETHAM, 1976

6. Marine Oil Pollution
   D. W. ABECASSIS, 1976

7. The Estates of Thorney and Crowland
   SANDRA RABAN, 1977

8. Peasant Movements in West Bengal
   SWASTI MITTER, 1977

9. Land, Planning and the Market
   B. J. PEARCE, N. R. CURRY, and R. N. GOOD-CHILD, 1978

10. Multiple Use of Woodlands
    M. R. CARROLL, 1978

11. Redistribution of Land Values: a re-examination of the 1947
    scheme
    H. L. LEUNG, 1979

12. Farm Modernisation and the Countryside
    F. G. STURROCK, and J. CATHIE, 1980

13. Land Management for Shooting and Fishing
    HELEN R. PIDDINGTON, 1981

14. Land Policy in Fiji
    D. T. LLOYD, 1983

15. West Midlands Farming, 1840s to 1970s
    G. M. ROBINSON, 1983

16. Land Compensation: A Study of Compensation
    Determination
    B. P. D. DENYER-GREEN, 1986

17. Private Rented Housing in the 1980s and 1990s
    C. M. E. WHITEHEAD and M. P. KLEINMAN, 1986

ABSTRACT

This study begins by examining why the private rented sector continues to be of interest to policy makers. It goes on to outline a series of hypotheses about current conditions within the sector, and the role which the sector performs in the overall housing system. These hypotheses are then confronted with the available evidence. Next, a forecast is made about the probable size and composition of the sector over the next 15 years. The important behavioural factors, on both the demand and supply sides, which are likely to affect the future development of the sector are identified and assessed.

The role that the sector might suitably play in an 'ideal' housing system which aimed to provide adequate accommodation for all, is then described. In this way what is likely to happen is compared to what might be desirable. This leads on to a discussion of the policy implications of the findings of the study, and to an assessment of the impact on the sector of changes to the legal framework.

ACKNOWLEDGEMENTS

This study forms part of a research project on structural change in the housing market funded by The Nuffield Foundation, to whom we are grateful for their continued assistance. We also wish to thank the external referees, Professor David Donnison of the University of Glasgow, and Michael Harloe of the University of Essex, and the two internal referees for their valuable comments and advice.

C. M. E. Whitehead
M. P. Kleinman

October 1986

Christine M. E. Whitehead is Senior Lecturer in the Department of Economics at the London School of Economics, and Senior Visiting Research Associate in the Department of Land Economy at the University of Cambridge. Mark Kleinman is a Research Assistant in the Department of Land Economy at the University of Cambridge.

CONTENTS

Page

LIST OF TABLES AND FIGURES

Chapter 1   WHY ARE WE INTERESTED IN THE
            PRIVATE RENTED SECTOR?
            1.1   Introduction 1
            1.2   Policy objectives of governments 7
            1.3   General hypotheses relating to condition...10
            1.4   General hypotheses about the role of the
                  sector 14

Chapter 2   CONDITIONS IN THE PRIVATE RENTED
            SECTOR
            2.1   Physical condition......................21
            2.2   Household characteristics 30
            2.3   Utilisation of the stock.................38
            2.4   Rent levels and contractual conditions.....40
            2.5   Rents in relation to income 47
            2.6   Equity between tenures 50
            2.7   Access to the sector ....:.54

Chapter 3   THE ROLE OF THE PRIVATE RENTED
            SECTOR IN THE HOUSING MARKET
            3.1   The demand for private renting 58
            3.2   The operation of the supply side 70
            3.3   The extent of pressure 84
            3.4   Conclusion with respect to the current
                  situation.............................87

Chapter 4   THE FUTURE OF PRIVATE RENTING
            4.1   Demographic-based projections 90
            4.2   Projections based on past trends.........97
            4.3   Synthesis 103

4.4 Behavioural factors 105

4.5 Supply factors 116

Chapter 5 WHO MIGHT THE SECTOR SERVE?

5.1 Renting versus owning................ 124

5.2 Private versus public renting........... 135

5.3 Who will and should the sector serve? ... 144

5.4 Sources of supply 148

Chapter 6 POLICY IMPLICATIONS AND
           CONCLUSIONS

6.1 Introduction 156

6.2 The choices available 158

6.3 An effective market 160

6.4 Problems of shortage 166

6.5 Additional controls 169

6.6 What should be done?................. 171

LIST OF TABLES

			Page
Table	1	Households and dwellings by tenure	2
	2	Dwellings built before 1919	22
	3	Unfitness and lack of repair by tenure	24
	4	Households lacking bath, inside W.C. or both	25
	5	Households in dwellings in multiple occupation	27
	6	Households sharing bath, inside W.C. or both	29
	7	Tenure by household type	31
	8	Tenure by usual gross weekly household income	33
	9	Households at densities more than 1 p.p. room	39
	10	Households at densities less than 0.5 p.p. room	39
	11	Gross rent and rates by tenure	42
	12	Median level of rent and rates by length of residence	45
	13	Weekly mortgage/rent as % of usual gross weekly income of head of household and wife by selected tenures	49
	14	New households: marital status and household type by tenure	59
	15	Households moving into PRS by household type	63
	16	Private renting and household type: stress areas and all England compared	64
	17	Household type by when letting commenced	65
	18	Satisfaction with accommodation by tenure and household type	69
	19	Accommodation most like to be living in, in two years time by age, marital status and present tenure	71
	20	Annual gross rates of return on capital values of DoE "Beacon" properties	79
	21	Propensity to be a private tenant by household type	91
	22	1981-based household projection, with constant propensities: England and Wales	92

23 Propensity to be a private tenant by age and household type: England 1981   93

24 1981-based projections, with constant propensities: England   94

25 Propensity to be a private tenant by age and household type: Greater London 1981   95

26 1981-based projections, with constant propensities: Greater London   96

27 Stock of PRS/HA dwellings, Great Britain: Observations 1972–1982, Projections for 1986, 1991, 1996, 2001   99

28 Non-linear GHS-based projections   100

29 Private renting households by household type 1971–82, projections for 1986, 1991, 1996, 2001   101

30 Projections by age and household type based on declining propensities   104

Chapter 1 Why are we interested in the private rented sector?

Introduction

The private rented sector continues to evoke interest at a level which in some ways seems quite out of proportion to its size. This concern comes from a wide range of sources including in particular:

> interest groups involved in trying to obtain better conditions for either landlords or tenants who are currently in the sector;
> local authorities and other organisations attempting to provide adequate accommodation for all types of households; employers and those looking for work who see the lack of readily available rented housing as a constraint on job mobility; and particularly
> central government and opposition parties who have strong and often conflicting view about the role that private renting should play within the housing system and the policies that might be employed to ensure that this role is effectively fulfilled.

Yet the private rented sector (PRS) now houses less than one in eight of all housholds (Table 1)[1] and indeed less than one in ten if we exclude letting by Housing Associations, which are really part of the social sector, and by employers, which serve a very different purpose. Moreover the importance of the sector has been in almost continuous decline since the early part of the century. In

TABLE 1

(a) *Households by tenure – England and Wales 1981*

	Thousands	Percent	% of PRS
Owner-occupiers	10,283	58	
Council/New Town	5,102	29	
Housing Association	361	2	
Total PRS	1,961	11	
– Business/Employment	374	2	19
– Unfurnished	1,077	6	55
– Furnished	510	3	26
ALL	17,706	100	

Source: 1981 Census

(b) *Dwellings by tenure – England 1981*

	Thousands	Percent
Owner-occupied	10,297	57
Council/New Town	5,056	28
Private Rented (including HA)	2,087	12
Vacant	626	3
ALL	18,066	100

Source: English House Condition Survey 1981

this context there is no direct evidence for the often quoted figure of 90% of the stock being privately rented in 1914 (Department of Environment 1977b and c) but undoubtedly private renting was the dominant tenure at that time. Even in 1938 it was still the majority tenure although the absolute number of units let privately in England and Wales had fallen from just over 7m in 1914 to 6.6m in 1938. Since the war the decline in both absolute and relative terms has been very rapid and there is no sign of its slowing down. During the 1970s the total number of households renting privately fell by one third, and by nearly one half if Housing Associations are excluded. As a result fewer than one and a half million households now rent privately. Given this decline one might perhaps expect that interest in the sector would be on the wane. In fact it has been maintained and possibly increased for reasons both to do with the economic and social problems related

2

to the sector and with the political context in which housing is provided.[2]

With respect to the first aspect there are two main reasons for this interest. On the one hand the conditions faced by many tenants and landlords are seen as being quite inadequate to meet acceptable housing standards. Equally, housing problems are generally seen as being concentrated in the private rented sector (Nevitt 1966, p. 9, Kleinman, 1984). On the other the sector is regarded as particularly important because of its role in allowing the overall housing market to operate effectively, especially in supplying easy access accommodation to new and moving households, and thus providing overall flexibility in the housing market which is difficult to achieve in the majority tenures.

These two features inter-relate both because of the way the housing system operates and because of government policy. In its access role the PRS acts as the market clearing tenure — because access to owner occupation and public sector housing is restricted. But, as the Department of Environment stated in 1977,

"the effect of any shortfall in the supply of housing, which is not absorbed by families living as concealed households, appears in the private rented sector. A margin of households over dwellings that is small when expressed as a proportion of the national housing stock is very much larger as a proportion of the stock in the private rented sector, and, larger still in relation to the 'accessible' private rented sector."

(Department of Environment, 1977a, p. 82)

As a result not only are problems of access to housing concentrated in the sector but they also adversely affect the conditions of those already living there.

In terms of the second aspect, there has been continuous government intervention in the PRS throughout the century. Of most direct importance is the fact that it has been subject to statutory rent controls and security of tenure since 1915, although

3

the form of these controls has varied over time. These controls mean that landlords have been forced to continue to provide accommodation at below market rents but also mean that landlords have had little or no incentive to maintain and improve their property or to provide additional accommodation to help those trying to enter the housing market. So policies aimed at providing adequate housing for those already living in the private rented sector may conflict with policies which aim to improve its operation within the housing market, because the first requires controls and the second is dependent on the sector being as unconstrained as possible.

This conflict is the major cause of the extent of political involvement in and dissension about the sector. The Conservative party and those with a more market-oriented ideological base argue that if general conditions in the housing market were improved and households given income-related assistance to purchase accommodation of an adequate standard, the PRS could be an effective means of providing rented units for the mobile and those who do not want or cannot afford to buy. The market-based approach therefore emphasises the conditions necessary to provide an economically viable rented sector — allowing freedom of contract between landlord and tenant and enabling those who seek rented accommodation to find it quickly and easily. The problems of low income and poor condition are then seen as being dealt with by income-related housing allowances rather than by social ownership.

Those on the left and particularly the Labour party, place far more stress on the poor conditions currently existing in the sector and at the limit argue that the relationship between a profit seeking landlord and a tenant is inherently unsuitable because the landlord must be in a position of relative power. Clearly those who hold this last view see no solution to housing problems within the private rented sector. However, even they recognise that it cannot be removed immediately and so people living in the sector must be helped. They also recognise that even if it were abolished certain underlying housing problems would remain and require solution elsewhere. In putting forward these policies they emphasise the importance of improving housing conditions for existing tenants and the existing stock. The question of providing additional new investment in rented housing and access to adequate housing are seen as separate issues to be solved through public intervention.

During most of the 1970s it was the view of the left that dominated. Rent controls were extended and incentives and powers to improve the existing stock were increased — and the sector continued to decline rapidly. Since the Conservatives returned to power although the ideological approach changed and there has been some legislation aimed at assisting the private rented sector,[3] the sector has continued to decline. There is now growing pressure from both within government and from a wide range of interest groups to try to reduce controls in an attempt to revive the sector. As a result the emphasis has moved away from concern with existing conditions to discussion of policies which might provide the incentives to increase investment and the provision of easy assess accommodation.

The immediate rationale of this change in emphasis comes from a number of sources. First there is considerable dissatisfaction with the way in which some parts of the public sector have been providing and managing their housing stock (Audit Commission 1986). Second, lack of easily accessible housing is thought to exacerbate the problems of the labour market and to restrict people's capacity to search for work and to accept job offers in other areas (Hughes and McCormick 1981). The growing imbalance of job opportunities between North and South has made this a more pressing issue in the 1980s. Third, it is argued that the range of choice available both to tenants and investors is limited by contraints on private renting and that freeing up the market would both improve conditions for those for whom owner occupation is not a suitable tenure and increase the amount of private finance going into the system and so expand overall investment. (National Federation of Housing Associations 1985b.)

This is linked politically with the government's general emphasis on privatisation (Whitehead 1984).

The vast majority of discussion about how the private rented sector operates, what problems are to be found there and what its role should be in the future takes place within this highly contentious political context. Perhaps as a result many of the statements and proposals that are put forward are not strongly based on available information about what the current situation is or what the effects of particular policies are likely to be. Yet before a coherent policy can even be specified, it is necessary to provide as clear as possible an explanation about how the private rented sector actually works and about the conditions prevailing in the sector, so that one can assess the likely costs and benefits of change.

In this text we hope to provide some of the material which will enable such an exercise to take place. To do this we first attempt to specify a series of hypotheses about the role and conditions of the sector. These hypotheses reflect generally accepted views of what is going on and are usually implicit in discussions about the sector. We then intend to confront each of these hypotheses with the currently available evidence to see to what extent our hypotheses are valid. In so doing we hope to provide a clear and strongly based starting point from which to examine both what is likely to happen given current policies and what might be done to improve the situation.

In the next section we make an attempt at forecasting the probable size of the sector over the rest of the century, and the sorts of households that are likely to become or remain private tenants, in the light of current demographic, economic and social trends. We then spell out what this implies for the likely future role of the sector, and ask whether this role is desirable from the point of view both of individual tenants and landlords and of housing policy overall. In this way we hope to compare what is likely to happen with what might be desirable. Finally we examine the policy implications of these comparisons and suggest in general terms the

way in which policy might be modified to improve the workings of
the sector.

Policy objectives of governments

Before specifying our hypotheses it is necessary to define some
sort of benchmark of acceptable standard both of housing
conditions and the operation of the housing system against which
our findings can be evaluated. In this way we can determine where
the evidence suggests that the private rented sector falls short of
meeting general housing aims. The most obvious starting point is
the set of policy objectives specified by succeeding governments.
In this context the provision of a decent home for every family at a
price within their means has been the stated policy of all post-war
governments.[4] The actual meaning of this phrase is of course
subject to interpretation and has over the years been modified
considerably as aspirations and therefore standards rise.

One important area of uncertainty which is particularly relevant
to the private rented sector is the definition of "every family". In
the early 1970's when *Fair Deal for Housing* was published, the
objective was indeed limited to families, i.e. households with
children. In the Housing Policy Review published in the mid
1970's the term family was retained but the context made it clear
that the objectives related not just to family households but also to
childless couples and many people living on their own. At the limit
it could be taken to include all persons who wish to live separately
whether or not they can afford to pay for that housing. A rather
more restrictive but widely accepted definition would exclude
younger single persons who are not themselves able to obtain
separate accommodation.[5] The private rented sector remains the
tenure to which many people with limited resources are restricted,
and to which many newly forming households are ineffectively
trying to gain entry. Therefore the definition which is accepted
will to a significant degree affect both our evaluations of whether
the PRS is carrying out its role in the housing market effectively

7

and whether the poor conditions faced by many tenants should be a subject of major concern to policy makers.

The definition of 'a decent home' is generally taken to refer mainly to conditions of the dwelling and the level of utilisation within the dwelling. It therefore includes:

- the provision of all standard amenities including adequate heating;
- adequate structural condition;
- the exclusive use of rooms and amenities if desired by the household;
- an acceptable amount of space per person taking into account the composition of the household in relation to the bedroom standard.

Over the last decade the definition has been extended to include rather wider concepts of suitability and access. Relevant factors with respect to the private rented sector here include:

- reasonable access to acceptable quality accommodation and the capacity to move house when circumstances, particularly employment, change;
- suitably designed and located dwellings for children, the elderly and others with special needs;
- a reasonable degree of freedom from interference by landlords in the way that tenants use their homes;

and many would argue

- security of tenure at least for longer term tenants.

It is generally accepted that many of those in the PRS do badly with respect to all these aspects of a decent home, and that indeed poor conditions are particularly concentrated in the sector. Further it is argued by some that the relationship between a private landlord and a tenant is inherently unsuitable so that again those in the PRS are particularly disadvantaged.

The third relevant area is 'at a price within their means'. This is generally taken to mean that housing costs should form a reasonable and stable proportion of household income. Twenty percent is often taken as an acceptable maximum although there is no formal basis for this value. Because of its role as a tenure of last resort and more generally as a tenure for lower income households, problems relating to ability to pay for adequate accommodation are thought to be concentrated in the private rented sector. Moreover income related assistance is argued to be least effective among private tenants because of high rents and low take-up levels.

Other housing objectives relate to equity both between households in similar circumstances and between tenures. Again the *Fair Deal for Housing* definition is a reasonable starting point. This stated that government objectives included 'a fairer choice between owning a home and renting one' and 'fairness between one citizen and another in giving and receiving help towards housing costs' (Department of Environment 1971, para 5).

During the 1970's greater emphasis was placed in discussion on freedom of choice with respect to tenure, on neutrality between tenures with respect to government assistance and on tenure neutral income-related subsidies (Lansley, 1979). Yet in reality the private rented sector continued to receive the least assistance while housing many of the poorest households, and access to other tenures remained restricted. And in the 1980's emphasis moved away from these ideas towards providing relatively greater assistance towards owner-occupation and towards access to that tenure especially by those in public sector housing. As a result those in the private rented sector could be regarded as being further disadvantaged.

Thus we suggest that there is a set of *overall* objectives for housing policy which is generally agreed with relatively minor differences between parties (although these areas of difference particularly affect the private rented sector) against which evidence about the sector can be evaluated. Further, it is generally accepted that it is within the private rented sector that many of the most difficult and persistent problems both of condition and operation will be found.

Hypotheses about the private rented sector

In the rest of this chapter we set out the main hypotheses about the current situation in the private rented sector which we wish to examine. To do this we look at the sector in two different ways – which reflect the different economic and political approaches set out above – and at the reasons why we expect these hypotheses to be valid.

First, we examine current conditions in the sector. Here the overall hypothesis is that conditions in the sector are both worse than those elsewhere in the housing system, and, in absolute terms, below socially acceptable minimum levels.

Second, we examine the sector's role in the housing system. This involves setting up a rather more complex set of hypotheses relating both to the heterogeneous nature of the sector and to the different perspectives of landlords and tenants.

In looking at these hypotheses it will often be relevant to distinguish between the three main sub-sectors (Table 1): the unfurnished sub-sector which is still the largest and provides mainly longer-term accommodation, the furnished which is where most easy access accommodation is to be found, and that held by virtue of employment which exists for quite different, job-related, reasons.

General hypotheses relating to condition

In looking at the conditions prevailing in the sector it is necessary to examine a number of different attributes relating to the characteristics of dwellings and households, to the utilisation of the stock, the terms and conditions under which it is rented, and the relative positions of tenants and potential tenants in comparison to others in the housing market.

Looking first at *physical conditions*, our general hypothesis is that private tenants live in poor conditions, that these conditions are consistently worse than those found in other sectors and that poor physical conditions are concentrated in the sector. There are a number of historical and physical factors which underlie this hypothesis. First, many of the dwellings in the sector are the same as when private renting was the majority tenure. They are therefore old and were built before amenities were standard. The unfurnished sector in particular includes a high proportion of older units with inadequate amenity. Further, because of the limited incentive to invest throughout much of the century, disrepair and unfitness are also thought to be concentrated in the sector. Second, the furnished sub-sector is made up of converted units or parts of other people's dwellings. These are more likely than average to be unsuitable for families and those with physical mobility problems and to have only shared amenities. Finally, one would expect job-related accommodation to be more modern and to have reasonable amenity.

With respect to *households* we expect to find disadvantaged households in the sector and this accounts for many of the problems relating to overcrowding, sharing, exploitation and high rent/income ratios. Among these are included in particular the elderly, who on average have low incomes and are likely to find it difficult to cope with housing problems. They are thought to be concentrated in the sector because they have been there throughout their lives and entered private renting when it was the majority tenure.

Immigrant households and to some extent migrants of all types are also thought to be over-represented because of various kinds of difficulties in entering the majority tenures, including problems of racial and other discrimination, inability to meet residence and other requirements, and lack of familiarity with 'the system'.

Perhaps most importantly, because those who can afford it will choose owner-occupation and access to public sector housing has in the past been difficult except for families and special needs groups, lower income non-family households are concentrated in the sector, particularly in unfurnished accommodation.[6] In addition, one can expect to find some family households who have not been able to obtain, or hold on to, accommodation in the majority tenures. Again, however, one would expect those in employment-related accommodation to have different characteristics – i.e. to be of working age and in employment and therefore likely to be family households with near-average incomes.[7]

These types of attribute[8] mean both that the capacity to pay of households in the sector is relatively low and that they may find difficulty in obtaining reasonable contractual conditions. With respect to *utilisation* these attributes are likely to imply that, apart from those whose household size has declined while living in that accommodation, tenants are likely to have relatively limited space per person. Thus in the unfurnished sector where adjustment has been restricted there will often be under-utilisation, while in the other parts of the sector households live at higher densities than elsewhere in the housing system.

Another important aspect of the limited bargaining power associated with low income, age and other disadvantages, relates to terms and conditions of the tenancy. Tenants may be unable to negotiate reasonable contracts because of their restricted choice. The problem does not exist in this form in owner-occupation because the landlord and tenant are the same person while in the public sector a major objective of social provision is to make sure that tenants obtain secure accommodation at a reasonable rent with an acceptable standard of management. Thus, this type of problem is concentrated in the private rented sector, particularly in those sub-sectors not subject to legislative controls on security and rent. They affect both *rent levels* which, when they are market determined, can be expected to be high both in absolute terms and in comparison to those in other sectors, and *security of tenure*. In this context there is thought to be significant avoidance and evasion of the Rent Acts, harassment of tenants and homelessness arising from eviction or contractual breakdown.

The combination of low incomes and often high rents leads to major problems of capacity to pay. In this context some tenants, although they pay high rents and obtain relatively poor value for money, will not be in financial difficulty because, for instance, they share the rent among a number of working members. On the other hand many tenants will find difficulty in paying even though the rent is low because their incomes are also extremely low. Even so the problem is thought to be concentrated in the less controlled parts of the sector, and to be made up of four element – high rents, low incomes, low take-up of benefits and difficulties just above the benefit level. In the parts of the sector that are more subject to controls, the problem is assumed to be rather different, made up of low rents, very low incomes and a heavy reliance on housing assistance, particularly supplementary pension, to enable the rent to be paid.

With regard to the question of more general *equity*, it is well understood that the policy of successive governments has favoured the majority tenures while those in the private rented sector have received no general subsidy. What subsidy there is arises from rent control and is therefore in the main a transfer from landlord to tenant (Department of Environment 1977c, Chapter 5; Whitehead 1980)[9]. This has major implications for the decisions of landlords and tenants, as well as for general equity, in that if either had a free choice they would often wish not to be involved in the sector. Thus both tenants and landlords are disadvantaged as against other tenures and other investments.

However the two major tenures both have significant constraints on access: owner-occupation in terms of ability to pay, to obtain adequate credit and to finance transaction costs, and the local authority sector in terms of waiting lists, allocation rules and the cutbacks in public expenditure. If these constraints remain, the provision of accommodation for every household can only be met through some households renting privately. However, limited supply, the resultant market rents, restricted availability of income-related subsidy and low take-up of that subsidy mean that *access* to private renting is also constrained and potential tenants are heavily disadvantaged. Evidence of access problems can be found by examining the extent and nature of homelessness, of involuntary concealed households, and of 'non-tenures' such as hostel and bed-and-breakfast accommodation.

This problem is clearly linked to the more general policy question of whether there is any desirable role for the private rented sector and, if so, whether it is currently able to fulfill such a role. It is therefore strongly related to the second group of general hypotheses.

General hypotheses about the role of the sector

In looking at the role of the sector we again examine a number of different attributes relating both to the types of household who one expects to find renting privately either through choice or because they can find nothing else, and to the types of landlord that provide this accommodation including those who might be prepared to continue to do so.

Looking first at *households* in the sector we suggest that private renting is the normal tenure for a number of groups of households including:

– newly forming and mobile households;
– older, usually non-family, households who have traditionally lived in the sector,
– non-traditional households of all ages, especially single people, who do not want to make a major commitment to housing;
– those whose work requires them to live on the premises or nearby;
– households who are unable to obtain accommodation in the majority tenures
        (House of Commons Environment Committee 1982a).

14

The first four roles are usually perceived of as necessary and desirable elements in the housing market with respect to which private renting may have relative advantages in comparison with other tenures. The final role is generally regarded as undesirable. However, such households require accommodation and this has not been made available in the majority tenures.

From the point of view of the policy maker it would be desirable to distinguish clearly between those who positively choose private renting because of its attributes as a tenure and those who are forced into private renting through lack of choice elsewhere. However, the distinction cannot readily be drawn from evidence of behaviour; all that can be done is to try to determine from the attributes of private renting the types of household most likely to find it attractive and those likely to find it unsuitable, perhaps supplementing this with evidence on stated preferences. The problem is exacerbated because choice depends on conditions within the private rented market and elsewhere. Thus, for instance, in a town where there is plenty of accommodation available a household may choose private renting because a desirable unit is available at the right price, and their decision to do this does not limit their future choice of options. In an area of housing stress a similar household may not be able to find the type of unit required and the high price paid may reduce the household's capacity to afford owner-occupation later.

The attributes associated with private renting which make it potentially desirable include the low costs of access in comparison to other tenures (for instance, it is usually only in private renting that a tenant can rent furniture and fittings), the lack of capital required, the limited time commitment involved and the lack of bureaucratic restrictions on access. Such attributes tend to be desirable to those just setting up house, those moving to new areas where they need time to evaluate other possibilities, those who expect to move fairly often and those who want to make only a limited commitment to housing.[10] Taking the obverse of these attributes it is likely to be undesirable for those who are looking for a long-term secure home which they can treat as they wish. Households wanting this type of accommodation would only be found in private renting because they are forced there by lack of opportunity elsewhere.

Our first general hypothesis therefore suggests that the private rented sector includes a high proportion of *younger mobile* households but that, especially in areas of housing stress, there are also likely to be concentrations of households who would be better served in the majority tenures and who are *forced* to rent privately.

The sector also plays a role in providing *longer term* accommodation particularly for older households. Here, private renting is thought to play a continuing role in providing accommodation for households who have traditionally regarded it as their usual tenure, acceptably meeting their long-term housing needs. In the main, this is seen as a residual role, housing those households who chose private renting when it was the majority tenure and who did not move on. By now such households are mainly pensioners. However, this group has been augmented over the years by younger, non-family, mainly lower-income households of all ages who rent for two quite different reasons: for some because the PRS is the most suitable tenure; and for others because, at least until recently, they had little chance of access to the majority tenures. Even today, although the local authority sector in particular has started to play a role in housing such households, the private rented sector is still regarded as the natural tenure for single people and non-family households of all types.

The final role relates to *job-related* accommodation. This role is thought to be restricted to a small number of types of employment where living in or near the premises is necessary, or where the employer requires the employee to move regularly as part of the job. The first includes mainly agricultural workers, together with the police, caretakers and others where the job is to oversee a particular location; the second relates mainly to the armed forces but also to the police to a lesser extent and to some construction

16

workers. Those in such accommodation are obviously mainly of working age and in employment. Their incomes might however be expected to be rather below the average both because their housing is usually provided free, and because some households with little choice and therefore market power either in terms of housing or jobs find themselves in this type of accommodation.

Thus in all three types of rented housing – easy access, long-term and job related – there will be some households who find themselves in the PRS who are *satisfied* with their accommodation and tenure because it provides the attributes they require, and others who are *dissatisfied* and would prefer the majority tenures.

So far our examination of how the role of the PRS within the housing market is perceived has concentrated on the demand side, to which indeed most policy discussion relates. However, the availability of accommodation to meet these requirements depends upon the preparedness of *landlords* to continue to let under the conditions they find in the market and to relet when their accommodation falls vacant. Those landlords who have provided accommodation for *long-term* sitting tenants are usually argued to be making a relatively low rate of return on their investment because of the effects of security of tenure and rent control legislation. Such landlords are generally expected to leave the sector when their property becomes vacant unless they have other reasons for letting, there are no alternative uses for the accommodation or they can let outside the Rent Acts and in so doing obtain an adequate return.

The position with respect to *new lets* is seen as even more problematic from the point of view of a healthy private rented sector. It is argued that for most landlords the rate of return available on new lettings is inadequate in comparison to that available on alternative investments. This is particularly so with respect to lettings within the Rent Act where 'fair rents' must be charged, but it is also argued to be the case for many landlords even if they are able to charge market rents. The main reason for

17

this is seen to be the relative advantage of the other tenures for the majority of households. This means that the rents obtainable are limited by the low capacity to pay of tenants remaining in the sector, while the price the landlord can obtain in the owner-occupied sector is enhanced. As a result it is thought that the sector may decline past the point at which it can serve a useful purpose as an easy access tenure.

Moreover, the types of property likely to remain will be those where the *rate of return* is relatively good. This probably applies mainly to: resident landlords (who only want a return on part of the dwelling); those letting dwellings in multiple occupation at high densities, particularly in areas of pressure, who can obtain a good rental income (since rents can be shared amongst several adults) in comparison to sale into single family occupation or properly converted flats; and poor quality accommodation especially where the demand even for owner-occupation is low. Further, because rent and security legislation reduces the rate of return, those interested in profitability will attempt to *avoid or evade* the Rent Acts as far as possible. This can fairly readily be achieved under current conditions through licence agreements,[11] company lets or holiday lets, or through tacit agreements between landlord and tenant. (House of Commons 1982a and c, Pearce 1982, Todd 1986). Thus rents for new lettings are mainly set by what the market will bear, in spite of rent controls, and few secure lettings are made available. These types of lettings are unlikely to be suitable for those looking for long-term accommodation.

It is further argued that the constraints on letting in the PRS are so great that the number of landlords prepared to let vacant property at all is too small for the many households seeking accommodation. Consequently, large numbers are unable to find anything they can afford, even given their eligibility for housing benefit. To this extent the sector is no longer fulfilling its easy access role, at least for lower income households. This, it is suggested, shows up in the growth of homelessness, particularly in London, and in the provision of accommodation in '*non-tenures*' such as hostel and bed-and-breakfast accommodation, as well as in a continuing problem of concealed households.

Overall it can be argued that the conditions under which the private rented sector now operates are not such that it is able to fulfil any of its roles effectively (House of Commons Environment Committee 1982a, para 99). To determine the reasons for this failure, its likely effect in the future and what might be done to improve its position requires a detailed analysis of each element of demand and supply and of how these come together to determine rents, availability and standards of accommodation.

In the next two chapters we therefore attempt to formulate these hypotheses about the private rented sector in rather more detail and to examine the empirical evidence in order to substantiate or modify the picture we have presented.

PRIVATE RENTED HOUSING IN THE 1980s AND 1990s

1. The 1981 Census showed 2.4 million households (13.1%) of the population) renting privately in England and Wales. Since then the decline, which had been running at about 100,000 households per year, appears to have continued.
2. For instance in the last decade the private rented sector has been examined officially in the Housing Policy Review (1974–76), the abortive Rent Act Review (1977–79), the House of Commons Select Committee on Environment (1980–82) and an internal review by the Department of the Environment (1983).
3. The most important are contained in the 1980 Housing Act which introduced two new forms of tenancy – shorthold and assured – involving fewer controls.
4. See, for example, Department of Environment (1971) and Department of Environment (1977a).
5. This is still a somewhat more generous definition than that currently in operation. The Housing (Homeless Persons) Act for instance imposes a duty on local authorities to secure accommodation for certain categories of homeless households, viz. families, pensioners, and some non-pensioner single people and couples who are deemed to be "vulnerable".
6. Although this does not exclude the possibility of higher income households choosing private renting at least for short periods.
7. This listing excludes single person households and groups of single people of working age who are an important part of the sector but do not normally cause concern.
8. Other attributes are discussed in detail later in relation to the question of the role of the sector in the housing market.
9. There is some element of subsidy from the taxpayer, in that, in the absence of control, part of the increased rent which a landlord could obtain would have been taxed as income.
10. The attributes of tenure will be discussed in more detail in Chapter 5 when we come to examine what the future role of the sector should be.
11. Though the recent judgement in *Street v Mountford* (*The Times*, 3/5/85) would appear to restrict the capacity of parties to avoid/evade the Rent Acts in this way.

Chapter 2   Conditions in the private rented sector

So far what we have done is to set out a number of generally-held views about the private rented sector. In order to evaluate these views we need to specify them more carefully so that they are in a form which makes it possible to test them with the available evidence. To do this we take each general area and break it down into a set of detailed hypotheses to which we can apply the available, mainly statistical, information in order to ascertain whether the stated views are valid. In this chapter we look at the hypotheses about conditions in the sector.

Physical condition

The first area of concern had to do with the physical condition of the stock which we hypothesised as being poor in comparison to other tenures and as including a high proportion of all the poor quality dwellings in the total stock. In this context we set up a number of more specific hypotheses and examine the relevant evidence.

1 i)   Older property is concentrated in the private rented sector.

About 1.3 million dwellings in the private rented sector in England in 1981 were built before 1919. This represents about 63% of all dwellings in the sector and about one-quarter of all pre-1919 dwellings (Table 2). However, over two-thirds of all pre-

TABLE 2

Dwellings built before 1919

Tenure	Thousands	Percent of all dwellings in the tenure (%)	Percent of all pre-1919 dwellings (%)	Percent of all occupied pre-1919 dwellings (%)
Owner-occupied	3356	33	64	69
Local authority/New Town	210	4	4	4
Private rented/Housing Association	1320	63	25	27
Vacant	383	61	7	–
ALL	5269	29	100	100

Source: 1981 English House Condition Survey Pt 1 Table 21

1919 units were owner-occupied. Thus, although a far higher proportion of the private rented sector is made up of older units than is the case in other sectors, the majority of such units are elsewhere, mainly in owner-occupation.

1 ii) Unfitness and disrepair are concentrated in the private rented sector, especially among unfurnished units.

More than one in six privately rented dwellings are unfit, a proportion which probably rises to one in five if Housing Association units are excluded. This compares with one in twenty in the owner-occupied sector and one in a hundred in the local authority sector (Table 3). Yet this still means that in absolute terms far more unfit units are owner-occupied than are rented. Vacant units also have a high propensity to unfitness although it is not known whether such units are awaiting repair or falling into dereliction.

Disrepair is relatively rather less concentrated in the private rented sector. However, even here a privately rented dwelling is twice as likely as an owner-occupied unit to require at least £2500 (in 1981 prices) spent on it to bring it up to reasonable condition, and where repairs are expected to cost more than £7000, that propensity increases to three times. Thus the majority of units that are unfit or in disrepair are to be found elsewhere, but a very significant minority of such units are privately rented (40% of occupied unfit units and 37% of those in serious disrepair among occupied units) and private tenants have a very high relative chance of suffering from poor housing conditions.

1 iii) Lacking amenity is concentrated in the sector.

In 1981 there were 579,000 households in England and Wales who lacked either bath or an inside WC or both (Table 4). 39% of these were private tenants, 86% of whom were in the unfurnished sector. Thus, while again the majority of households lacking amenity live in other tenures, mainly in the owner-occupied

TABLE 3

Unfitness and lack of repair by tenure
(thousands of dwellings and percentages)

	Unfit			Repair costs over £7000*			Repair Costs over £2500*			
	Number (000s)	% Tenure	% Unfit	Number (000s)	% Tenure	% Needing Repair	Number (000s)	% Tenure	% Needing Repair	All Dwellings
Owner-occupied	483	5	43	539	5	51	2189	21	56	10297
LA/New Town	67	1	6	50	1	5	608	12	16	5056
Privately rented (including HA)	370	18	33	343	16	33	875	42	22	2087
Vacant	196	31	18	117	19	11	247	40	6	626
ALL TENURES	1116	6	100	1049	6	100	3919	22	100	18066

Source: English House Condition Survey 1981, Tables 13 and 21

*Note that dwellings in disrepair may also be unfit and vice versa. Overall the evidence suggests that perhaps 78% of unfits require repairs costing more than £2500 and 43% over £7000. The overlap is therefore very great but not complete.

TABLE 4

Households lacking bath or inside W.C. or both, England and Wales 1981

	Thousands	% of all households lacking	% of all households in the tenure
Owner-occupiers	255	44	2
Public sector	98	17	2
Private rented: all	227	39	12
– unfurnished	196	34	18
– furnished	22	4	4
– business/employment	9	2	2
ALL TENURES	579	100	3

Source: Census HH 1981, Table 10

sector, a very large minority are in one particular part of the privately rented sector – and in this sub-sector nearly one in five households lack one (or both) of the two most basic amenities.

There is considerable overlap between the three attributes of poor quality – unfitness, disrepair and lacking amenity – which we have discussed so far. For instance, 78% of unfit units required repairs of over £2500 in 1981 (Department of Environment 1982, Table 28). Moreover, all three attributes are highly correlated with the age of the dwellings. As a result, the majority of units in the private rented sector in England (55%) are either unfit, or require more than £2500 (at 1981 prices) spent on repairs, or lack amenity. Many of these come under two or more categories. Further, a very high proportion are in the unfurnished sector. Poor dwelling condition is thus relatively very highly concentrated in the private rented sector and the majority of households renting from private landlords suffer from these conditions. However, because of the small size of the sector, particularly relative to owner-occupation, in no instance are the majority of dwellings suffering from a given condition privately rented.

1 iv) Non-self-contained accommodation and dwellings in multiple occupation are concentrated in the sector.

The private rented sector houses the absolute majority of households living in accommodation which is either not self-contained or has a shared entrance (Table 5). Indeed, the absolute majority of non-self-contained units are in the furnished sub-sector and more than three-quarters of all such households rent privately. Most of those who live in non-self-contained accommodation in the majority tenures probably do so because they sub-let. If we include households whose accommodation is self-contained but who share an entrance, then the concentration in the PRS is not so great, although well over a third are in the furnished sub-sector, and 60% rent privately (Table 5).

1 v) Sharing accommodation and amenity is concentrated in the private rented sector especially in the furnished sub-sector.

Although only 4% of households share any part of their home, over 70% of these households are to be found in the private rented sector (Rauta 1986, Table 2.2). The majority of these households (40%) live in furnished accommodation, although sharing only hallways and landings was more often found among unfurnished tenancies.

Sharing amenity is highly concentrated in the private rented sector in both absolute and relative terms. More than two-thirds of all who share amenity are private tenants (Table 5) and three-quarters of these are in the furnished sub-sector. The problem is thus even more concentrated than lack of self-containment and sharing accommodation – and affects more than one in four of all households in furnished accommodation.

Hence the problems of sharing are seen to be absolutely concentrated in a very small sub-sector of the total housing stock, accounting for less than 3% of all households.

1 vi) The proportion of households with central heating is lower than in other tenures.

TABLE 5

Households in dwellings in multiple occupation

	Households in non-self-contained accommodation			Households in accommodation either non-self-contained or with shared entrance		
	No. (000s)	% of those in that tenure	% in non-self-contained accommodation	No. (000s)	% of those in that tenure	% in non-self-contained/ shared entrance accommodation
Owner-occupied	37	–	16	158	2	21
LA/New Town	18	–	8	135	2	18
PRS						
– unfurnished	51	5	22	161	25	22
– furnished	125	25	53	270	53	37
– business/employment	3	1	1	14	4	2
PRS total	180	9	77	444	23	60
TOTAL ALL HOUSEHOLDS	235	1	100	737	4	100

Source: Census HH 1981, Table 6

27

This is one of the few measures of quality as opposed to poor condition that is available. It reflects the age of the dwelling and the level of expenditure that both owner and occupier are prepared to make on housing. Nearly 60% of households had central heating by 1981 but only 38% of furnished tenants and 22% of those living in unfurnished accommodation benefited (O.P.C.S. 1983a, Table 3.36). Thus overall only about one in four of private tenants have central heating in their dwellings.

1 vii) Only in accommodation related to employment are physical conditions consistently adequate.

It is not always possible to distinguish accommodation let with employment from the rest of the private rented sector. However, where it can be done, conditions are markedly better than elsewhere in the sector and indeed no worse than for the stock as a whole. A far higher proportion has been built since 1919, fewer than 2% lack one or both of the two basic amenities (Table 4), and only 4% share an entrance or live in non-self-contained units (Table 5). Thus tenants living in accommodation related to their employment undoubtedly fare far better than others in the private rented sector and their housing is generally of an acceptable standard.

The evidence on physical condition produces a fairly clear picture. A majority of households in the unfurnished sector live in accommodation which does not meet reasonably acceptable standards and a large majority of those in the furnished sector do not have fully separate accommodation. So policies aimed at alleviating those conditions would, if successfully implemented, benefit a high proportion of private tenants. Tenure specific policies to alleviate these conditions would be more easily directed at the relevant problems in the private rented sector than elsewhere because of this relative concentration. However, if the aim is to alleviate specific conditions wherever these are found, it would generally be more relevant to concentrate on the owner-

28

TABLE 6

Households sharing bath, inside W.C. or both

England and Wales 1981

	Thousands	% of all sharing households	% of all households in the tenure
Owner-occupiers	31	12	0
Public sector	45	18	1
Private rented: all	172	69	9
– unfurnished	34	14	3
– furnished	134	54	26
– business/employment	4	2	1
ALL TENURES	247	100	1

Source: Census HH 1981, Table 10

occupied sector where the largest number of units that are unfit, lack amenity or require significant repair are to be found. Thus only if *relative* concentration is regarded as important, either because it implies greater suffering or because it can be alleviated at less cost, is it sensible to direct policies to alleviate physical conditions specifically at the private rented sector. Indeed, if the objective is simply to enable as large a number of households as possible to reach a given standard it will be more effective to concentrate help on owner-occupation both because more problems are to be found there and because the level of take-up of subsidies is likely to be higher among owner-occupiers than among renters or their landlords.

These arguments do not apply with respect to self-containment and sharing of amenity which are both relatively and absolutely concentrated in the furnished sub-sector. However, to a great extent these are attributes of that type of tenure and only by restricting the number of lettings could they be removed. Policies here can be extremely tenure specific – but the costs of losing some types of accommodation suitable for certain groups of household would have to be taken into account.

29

Household characteristics

The second relevant area relates to the types of household found in the sector. Here we hypothesise that elderly households are concentrated in unfurnished accommodation, that the young and the mobile are likely to be found in the furnished sub-sector and that overall it is a sector for those with low incomes and few other opportunities.

2 i) Pensioner households are concentrated in private renting, especially in the unfurnished sub-sector.

Single pensioner households account for 28% of all households in the unfurnished sub-sector, twice the proportion in the population as a whole (Table 7). Two-person pensioner households are also over-represented (23% as opposed to 15%). Thus the majority of households in the unfurnished sub-sector are of pensionable age. However, in the sector as a whole this concentration is offset by the low proportion of elderly households in the furnished and employment-related sub-sectors. Single pensioners are still over-represented in the PRS as a whole (18% as against 14% of all tenures) although such households are somewhat more concentrated in the public sector. Two-person elderly households are spread evenly across the three tenures. Thus it is true that elderly households are heavily concentrated in the unfurnished sub-sector and that the single elderly are particularly strongly represented. However, a higher proportion of both types of elderly household are to be found in the public sector than in the private rented sector as a whole.

The heavy concentration of elderly households in the rented sector has always been explained by reference to the usual tenure of the cohort, i.e. at the time when these households first entered the housing market, private renting was the predominant tenure. The difference between the tenure structure of two-person and single person households can be accounted for in two ways: the single who are survivors of married couple households are likely to

TABLE 7

Tenure by household type – England and Wales 1981

	All H/H	Owner occu- piers	Public sector	Total PRS	Unf.	Furn.	Bus./ Empt.
Without children							
1 adult pensionable age	14	11	19	18	28	8	2
2 adults at least 1 pens. age	15	15	16	15	23	3	7
1 adult < pens. age	8	6	7	18	11	40	8
2 adults < pens. age	16	18	12	18	13	27	21
incl. married couple	(12)	(15)	(9)	(11)	(9)	(10)	(18)
not incl. married couple	(3)	(3)	(3)	(7)	(4)	(16)	(3)
3 or more adults	14	15	13	10	9	9	15
incl. married couple	(12)	(13)	(11)	(7)	(7)	(2)	(14)
not incl. married couple	(2)	(2)	(2)	(3)	(2)	(7)	(2)
Total without children	67	65	67	79	84	87	53
With children							
Married couple	21	25	16	14	10	8	34
2 other adults	2	1	3	1	1	1	1
3 or more adults	9	9	9	5	4	2	11
1 adult	2	1	4	1	2	2	1
Total with children	33	36	32	21	17	13	47
ALL HOUSEHOLDS	100	100	100	100	100	100	100

Source: 1981 Census HH, Table 21

31

be older than those in two-person households and so belong to a cohort even more likely to have rented all their lives. Secondly, those who have always lived alone are more likely to rent than to own, in any cohort. In addition, elderly owner-occupiers, when they find themselves alone, may technically become renters, by moving to live with their children. The relative weights that should be given to these elements are important for forecasting the future tenure structure, but little evidence is available to determine these weights.

2 ii) Low-income households are concentrated in the private rented sector, particularly in unfurnished accommodation.

Evidence on incomes is obtained from voluntary surveys so there are usually a significant number of refusals and the results are not normally as accurate as for other attributes. Further, it is particularly difficult to obtain the correct representation of furnished tenants. The best source which can be broken down by sub-sector is the General Household Survey. This shows that in 1981 lower-income households were heavily over-represented in the unfurnished sub-sector with 13% of all households with incomes below £30 per week and 14% of those below £40 in 1981 located there. However, only the very lowest income group was over-represented in the furnished sub-sector (Table 8). Those with accommodation related to employment did not generally have low incomes – indeed, both their mean and median incomes were above the overall average (Table 8). In the unfurnished sub-sector, median income was only just above half (and the upper quartile only two-thirds) that for all households. The income of furnished tenants, although higher, was still below the general average with both median and upper quartile being a little over 80% of the level for all households.

Part of this concentration in the unfurnished sub-sector can be explained by the high proportion of pensioner households. Semi-skilled workers are only slightly over-represented in the private

TABLE 8

Tenure by usual gross weekly household income

Great Britain 1981

	With job/ business £	Private Rented Sector		All households £
		Unfurn. £	Furn. £	
Mean income	158	91	120	140
Lower quartile	89	40	58	57
Median income	137	63	98	120
Upper quartile	196	123	153	190
	%	%	%	%
Mean income as % of "all households" mean	113	65	86	100
Median income as % of "all households" median	114	53	82	100

Source: General Household Survey 1981, Table 3.11(b)

rented sector and the unfurnished sub-sector, but 56% of unfurnished tenants are economically inactive as compared to 34% of all households (O.P.C.S. 1984). However, the Family Expenditure Survey which breaks down income information by economic activity suggests this is only a partial explanation. In this survey, incomes of economically active unfurnished tenants were only 75% of the overall average, while those of the inactive were 78% (Department of Environment 1983c, Table 12.2). Thus, although the median income of unfurnished tenants is brought down by the age mix of the tenure, this does not provide a full explanation. Moreover, it is clear that working tenants in unfurnished accommodation earn significantly less than similar tenants in local authority accommodation.

An equivalent break-down cannot be obtained for tenants of furnished accommodation. It is therefore impossible to exclude those without employment to determine whether it is the higher

33

proportion of inactive households which explains the lower average income. Some evidence on socio-economic mix from the Private Rented Sector 'follow-up' survey (Todd et al. 1982) suggests that it is likely to be an important element. However, the low proportion of pensioner households would suggest that it is unlikely to be a complete explanation.

Thus, overall, households on low incomes are relatively concentrated in private renting and particularly in the unfurnished sub-sector. Some of this concentration can be related to age and economic inactivity, but these are not the only reasons.

2 iii) Moving households, especially those who have come some distance or from abroad, are concentrated in the private sector, especially in the furnished sub-sector.

While the private rented/Housing Association sector accounted for only 13% of all households in 1981, 23% of those who had moved in the year prior to the Census had moved into private renting. Evidence from the NDHS follow-up survey showed that the furnished sub-sector was relatively by far the most important sector in which movement occurred. Accounting for less than 3% of all households, it contained 16% of movers (O.P.C.S. 1983b, Table 2.1). Further, the Labour Force Survey in 1981 showed that 50% of tenants in the furnished sub-sector had moved in the past year (O.P.C.S. 1982). Movement into and within the unfurnished sub-sector on the other hand was at a level similar to the national average.

Secondly, the greater the distance moved the more likely was the household to find accommodation in the private rented sector. Indeed, among those entering England and Wales from outside Great Britain, the proportion finding private rented accommodation was as high as 63% (O.P.C.S. 1983c).

Mobility can either be a result of choice or can be forced on households by their housing and other circumstances. Evidence from the NDHS follow-up survey on Recently Moving Households (O.P.C.S. 1983b) suggests that long-distance moves into the private rented sector are most common among those moving from owner-occupation or local authority accommodation. Such households are likely mainly to be moving from choice and are not a matter of concern. However, evidence, particularly from Todd et al. (1982), suggests that movers into the PRS are likely to face worse conditions than those faced by existing tenants. In particular, rents are higher, the extent of security is less, sharing and overcrowding are greater.[1] The extent of movement into the sector and the housing that movers-in obtain are therefore a matter of concern (as well as of importance with respect to the easy access role of the sector discussed in the next section).

2 iv) Households from the New Commonwealth are more likely to find accommodation in the private rented sector than elsewhere.

The 1981 Census shows 15% of households where the head of household was born in the New Commonwealth or Pakistan to be in the PRS or HA sectors, as compared to 13% of all households. The proportion in the sector is below the overall average for the three main groups – from the Caribbean, India and Pakistan – and is only significantly higher than average for those from Bangladesh, the Far East and for the unspecified category. Taken together with the evidence on migration (above), this suggests that the private rented sector is likely to be the first home of new immigrants but those who settle here are as likely as the indigenous population to find accommodation in other tenures.

2 v) Some family households are forced into the sector.

As specified, this cannot readily be tested unless a survey includes detailed questions on preferences and reasons for moving. However, there are some indications. First the proportion of households with children in the sector is now relatively low – 21% as against 33% of all households (Table 7). Breaking that number down into sub-sectors, we find that these households are

35

concentrated in accommodation related to employment – where almost half the households include children. In the traditional private rented sector there are fewer than 250,000 households with children. Thus private renting unrelated to employment is not the usual tenure for family households. However, the proportion of single-parent households in both furnished and unfurnished accommodation was 2%, the same as in the population as a whole. This could imply difficulty of access, especially into owner-occupation, or it may reflect the likelihood that there is a higher than average proportion of recent movers among this group. More generally, the NDHS follow-up survey (O.P.C.S. 1983b) suggests that family households were more likely to have been recent movers than non-family households in the sector.

The BSA survey on tenure choice found few people among the general population who wished to live in the private rented sector in two years' time – 1% in the furnished and 3% in the unfurnished sub-sectors. This suggests that a large number of households of all types who do not want to live in private rented accommodation are forced to do so, but that this is not particularly concentrated among family households.

Evidence with respect to family households thus suggests that the numbers in the traditional sub-sectors are very low. However, the propensity among one-parent families is considerably higher. Other evidence, particularly on income related to household type, would be necessary to determine whether those family households that remain in the sector are particularly likely to have been forced to choose private renting.

2 vi) The household structure of those in accommodation rented with employment is similar to that for all households of working age.

The vast majority of those in the employment-related sub-sector are of working age. However, as compared to the general working-age population, there is a somewhat higher proportion of all households with children (Table 7). That is, the profile of the employment-related sub-sector is more like that of the owner-occupied sector for those of working age, than like that of the population as a whole.

Hence, overall the household structure observed in the private rented sector is consistent with the generally-held view. However, there are certain differences, some of which are of relevance to policy formulation.

First, it is only single pensioners who are heavily concentrated in the sector. This could mean that as, over time, the very elderly increasingly become the survivors of married couple households who have been located in the majority tenures, the demand for private renting will decline more rapidly. However, it also means that many of those in the unfurnished sector are the most vulnerable households in need of a wide range of social services. Second, the evidence on income suggests that tenants' capacity to pay is indeed low throughout the sector and that even those who are working are at the lower end of the earning scale. Again, this implies that some households are likely to be vulnerable and to require assistance from a wide range of services. However, it is not easy to pinpoint concentrations of household types in particularly poor circumstances: families are heavily under-represented except in the employment-related sub-sector; there is little evidence of significant concentrations of New Commonwealth households, except possibly among those newly arrived in Britain; and the relatively large numbers of single-parent households may also be related to their mobility as well as their vulnerability. More generally, the private rented sector does indeed cater for mobile households including those from other sectors moving some distance, but its absolute importance in this respect is undoubtedly declining (see Chapter 3 below). Finally, it is important to note that those in accommodation related to employment have characteristics very different from the rest of the sector – being mainly of working age, often with children and with incomes somewhat above the overall average.

Utilisation of the stock

Because of the different regimes that apply in the different sub-sectors, the level of utilisation can be expected to vary between these and between the private rented sector and the rest of the stock. Detailed hypotheses include:

3 i) Overcrowding is concentrated in the private rented sector, especially in the furnished sub-sector and among those who have recently moved.

Overcrowding is not concentrated in the private rented sector as a whole. Indeed, households are more likely to be overcrowded in the public sector (Table 9a). However, in the furnished sub-sector about 7% of households live at a density of more than one person per room, which is a significantly higher proportion than in other tenures. Further, the furnished sub-sector has the lowest proportion living at less than 0.5 persons per room (Table 10). Evidence from the NDHS follow-up survey suggests that movers are somewhat more likely to be overcrowded than non-movers in the private rented sector (Table 9b), and that overcrowding among movers is relatively high in the sector. The 1978 Private Rented Sector Survey (PRSS) similarly showed that recent movers had less room per person than longer-term residents. For instance, 12% of movers had accommodation below the bedroom standard, as opposed to 8% of all lettings (Todd et al. 1982, Table 4.14).

3 ii) Under-utilisation can be expected to be concentrated in the unfurnished sub-sector, especially among long-term tenants.

The majority of households in the country (56%) now live at a density of less than 0.5 persons per room which is the lowest level analysed (Table 10). However, that figure rises to 71% in the unfurnished sub-sector, giving it by far the highest level of under-utilisation. This is partly because densities are negatively

TABLE 9

Overcrowding: Households at densities more than 1 p.p. room

(a) *All households*   England and Wales 1981

	Number	As % of all h/hs in that tenure	As % of all crowded h/hs
Owner-occupied	221 282	2	37
Public sector	299 449	5	50
Total PRS	73 677	4	12
– unfurnished	26 436	2	4
– furnished	33 686	7	6
– business/employment	13 555	4	2
TOTAL	594 408	3	100

Source: Census HH 1981, Table 6

(b) *Moving households*

	As % of all movers in that tenure	As % of all overcrowded movers
Owner-occupied	1	17
Public sector	5	38
PRS (inc. HA)	5	47
TOTAL	4	100

Source: 'Recently Moving Households', Table 4.5

TABLE 10

Under-utilisation: Households at densities less than 0.5 p.p. room

England and Wales 1981

	Thousands		As % of all under-utilising households	As % of all households in that tenure
Owner-occupied	6087		61	59
Public sector	2686		27	49
PRS	1167		12	60
– unfurnished		767	8	71
– furnished		224	2	44
– business/employment		177	2	47
ALL TENURES	9940		100	56

Source: Census HH 1981, Table 6

correlated with length of residence.[2]

Yet, it should be remembered that in absolute terms the vast majority of both overcrowding and under-utilisation is to be found in other tenures, overcrowding mainly in the public sector and under-utilisation mainly in owner-occupation (Tables 9a & 10).

3 iii) There is some overcrowding among tenants renting accommodation with employment.

4% of households renting with their job live at a density greater than one person per room – a figure somewhat above the national average (Table 9a). Also, only 47% live at densities less than 0.5 persons per room (Table 10). There is therefore some evidence that these households obtain less than the average amount of space. However, there is no evidence of significant mismatch arising from the linking between job and home.

Overall, overcrowding has become of relatively minor importance at the national level. However, it is relatively concentrated among those in the furnished sub-sector and among recent movers. In policy terms, if it is intended to alleviate crowding specifically within the private rented sector, tenants' capacity to pay would have to be increased to the point where they could afford an adequate standard. If the objective instead is to reduce the number of households that are overcrowded as much as possible, policy should be concentrated on public sector allocation and transfer rules, as well as increasing provision of larger units in the public sector.

Rent levels and contractual conditions

The private rented sector can be subdivided into three main sub-sectors from the point of view of rent levels: the first is where control is formally organised – that is, where rents are registered; the second where, although the potential for registration exists, rent is determined by agreement between landlord and tenant; and the third where rents are determined outside the Rent Acts –

including both tenancies which are specifically excluded by the legislation and those where the contract is specified to avoid or evade the Acts. Rents in the first sub-sector are set below the market clearing level except where there is no shortage. On average, those in the second might be expected to be below market levels because they are theoretically subject to the same legislation, although some will clearly be market determined. Those in the third can be expected to be market determined.[3] Moreover, it is argued that such rents will be higher than payments for equivalent accommodation in other tenures because of the effect of controls on supply, the difficulties that tenants face in obtaining accommodation in other tenures and the subsidies available elsewhere. Further, the degree of control is thought to be related to the length of tenancy as rent control and security of tenure are strongly linked in the legislation. In the free market, rents are also usually related to the length of residence if only because of inertia.

Detailed hypotheses therefore include:

4 i) Rent levels are related to the extent of legislative security.

Regular information on rents relates only to housing expenditure in the furnished and unfurnished sub-sectors. It does not relate directly to the level of security nor does it standardise for size and quality. However, we do know that weekly expenditure in the furnished sub-sector averaged £24.18 in 1983, as compared to £16.54 in the unfurnished (Table 11). Tenants in the furnished sub-sector generally have smaller accommodation and often share amenity and live in property which is in a poor state of repair. Adjustment cannot be formally made for these differences but it is probably reasonable to assume those in the furnished sub-sector are paying at least twice as much. Evidence from the PRSS where tenancies were categorised by the way rents were determined supported the hypothesis, showing rents to be negatively correlated with the extent of control (Todd et al. 1982). Average size of accommodation was similarly negatively correlated. Not

TABLE 11

Gross rent and rates by tenure

United Kingdom 1983

	£
Local authority rented	19.18
Private rented – unfurnished	16.54
Private rented – furnished	24.18
Owner-occupied – in process of purchase	25.32
Owner-occupied – owned outright	22.29
Rent-free	16.36
ALL TENURES	22.07

N.B. For owner-occupied/rent-free tenures, gross rent is imputed value of the rental equivalent.

Source: Family Expenditure Survey 1983, Annex B, Table A, p.109.

only were registered rents lower than others, but average unregistered regulated rents were lower than those in the resident landlord sector – suggesting that the framework of security and control affects rent determination even where the formal procedures are not observed.

Evidence presented to the Select Committee on the Environment by the Law Centres Federation and the Wandsworth Legal Resource Project gave examples of the rents of similar flats where the free market rent was £46.15 as compared to the registered fair rent of £11.50, and licensees were paying rents three times those for fair rented accommodation in the same block (House of Commons Environment Committee 1982c, p. 45). Moreover, a survey by the Greater London Council of 2000 private tenants in London in 1983-4, which distinguished between 'protected' and 'unprotected' occupiers, showed that the average rent per room per week for protected tenants was £7.64, while for unprotected tenants it was £23.29 (Greater London Council 1985, para 40). Thus there seems no doubt that rents are related to the degrees of control and that in areas of shortage the differences are very large.

4 ii) Rent levels are higher in the uncontrolled sector than for comparable property in other tenures.

There are two aspects to this question: (a) do tenants receive worse value for money than those in other tenures? and (b) is the return obtained on letting higher than that achievable elsewhere in the housing market? With respect to the first: those in the unfurnished sub-sector on average pay a low rent for poor quality accommodation. The rent is, for instance, usually lower than in the public sector (Table 11) but the quality is also lower. In the furnished sub-sector tenants pay considerably above the average for all tenures while the quality of accommodation obtained is far below. The quality of services or furniture provided is very unlikely to be enough to offset these differences. The evidence therefore suggests those in the controlled sector usually pay little for little, while those in the less controlled part of the sector obtain very poor value for money in comparison to households elsewhere. This view was strongly borne out by landlord associations and others giving evidence to the Select Committee (House of Commons Environment Committee 1982a, para 58). Furthermore, our analysis of the GLC's evidence on rents in London shows that the average weekly rent for a privately rented unfurnished one-bedroom flat was £17.54, compared with £14.21 for a one-bedroom council flat (GLC 1986).

Direct evidence on rates of return is far more difficult to obtain. Rent levels suggest that unless the costs of providing accommodation are extremely high, returns in some uncontrolled parts of the sector must be very large in comparison to alternative housing uses. The Department of Environment 'Beacons' survey on rates of return on registered rents suggests that in areas where there is thought to be little excess demand, rents are set at between 4% and 6% of capital value (Department of Environment 1985a). In areas of shortage, especially in Greater London, rents cover only about 2–3% of capital value. This difference is certainly less than the differences in rents observed between fair rents and market rents in London – which might give a rent to capital value

43

rate of 5-10% excluding extreme examples (Mitchell 1985; Whitehead and Kleinman 1986). Thus, indirect and inconclusive as it is, evidence again suggests that some rates of return in the uncontrolled sector are significantly above the return required elsewhere.

4 iii) Rents are inversely related to the length of time that the tenant has lived in the accommodation.

Evidence on rents in relation to length of residence comes mainly from the PRSS. Table 12 shows clearly that in both furnished and unfurnished sub-sectors rents are higher the shorter the period of occupancy. Longer-stay tenants appear to obtain a better deal in both the market and controlled sectors. Analysis of the GLC data shows a very similar pattern for London in the early 1980s. Among 'recent lettings' (defined as those commencing within the previous four years) average rents were 15% higher compared with all lettings in the furnished sub-sector, and 54% higher in the unfurnished sub-sector (GLC 1986).[4]

Thus the evidence on rents suggests that the legislative framework has a significant effect on average rent levels where informal rent setting procedures are utilised. It further suggests that in the less controlled parts of the sector tenants receive very poor value for money and that those who move obtain a worse deal than those who are able to remain in their accommodation. It is not clear how those in the more controlled part of the sector fare in terms of value for money because, although they pay low rents, they also obtain a low level of services; so low, indeed, that it is reasonable to assume that they do badly in comparison to public sector tenants.[5] Finally, it seems reasonable to suggest from the range of evidence that many freely-determined rents in areas of stress are significantly higher than would obtain if supply were not adversely affected by controls and if tenants were able to choose freely between tenures. Thus the general hypothesis that tenants are often unable to bargain effectively with landlords to obtain a

Table 12

Median level of rent and rates for accommodation by length of residence

England 1978

Year of letting commencement*	Furnished			Unfurnished		
	England £	London £	Rest of England £	England £	London £	Rest of England £
1957 or before				4.50	6.60	4.10
1958 to 1967				5.30	7.00	4.80
1968 to 1974	9.60	11.10	7.90	6.20	8.90	5.40
1975 to 1976	12.00	16.50	9.40	7.20	9.20	6.70
1977 to 1978	13.90	21.20	11.20	9.00	11.30	8.30

* excluding rent-free
Source: Todd et al., The Privately Rented Sector in 1978, Table 5.7

reasonable contract in comparison to those available elsewhere appears correct.

4 iv) There is evidence of avoidance and evasion of the Rent Acts and of homelessness arising from the loss of accommodation.

The Environment Committee, after taking evidence from over one hundred and fifty witnesses, concluded that a large proportion of new lettings, especially in London, were either formally or practically outside the Rent Act. Some witnesses indeed reported that virtually all new lets were of this type (House of Commons Environment Committee 1982a, 1982b, 1982c). Longer-term lets are far more likely to be protected: while some 30% of all lettings in 1978 were subject to either controlled or registered rents, this proportion fell to only 13% of the most recent lettings (those commencing in 1977 or 1978) compared to more than three-quarters of lettings that began more than 30 years before (Todd et al. 1982 Table 3.2).

The 1983/84 GLC survey, which was undertaken mainly to assess the extent of the problem of avoidance and evasion, found that two-thirds of tenants were probably protected, but these were concentrated among longer-term tenants. Among those whose tenancies began in 1980 or after, only about one-third appeared to be protected. In addition, the survey found that 5% of tenants had recently suffered some form of substantial harassment, and the incidence of harassment was significantly higher in Central London than in the outer boroughs (GLC 1985).

23% of families accepted by District Councils as homeless in 1978 came from the private rented sector – nearly 40% of these from accommodation related to employment (*Housing and Construction Statistics*, June 1980, Table 2.27). While this means that more homeless families came from the private rented sector than either of the majority tenures, they are nevertheless far fewer than the numbers of homeless families who had never had a separate home (see also 7 (iii) below). More detailed evidence, which used a wider definition of homelessness, found that nearly one-third of homeless households in 1981 came from private renting. But the proportion had fallen from over 50% ten years before, as the importance of private renting in the total stock declined (Austerberry, Schott and Watson 1984, Table 5.4).

The evidence thus bears out the hypotheses that many who live in the private rented sector face insecurity and possible harassment, and that these problems are concentrated among those who have lived in their accommodation for a short time. Longer-term tenants, while by no means always formally secure, generally have better contractual conditions.

Rents in relation to income

We have suggested that it is not just rent levels and contractual conditions which are perceived to be the source of difficulty in the PRS but rather these elements taken in conjunction with income levels. Data on the extent of hardship are limited, and come mainly from irregular surveys. The last detailed material relates to 1979.

We can specify our hypotheses in more detail as follows:

5 i) Households paying more than 20% of their income in housing costs are concentrated in the private rented sector and particularly in furnished accommodation.

Even when income-related assistance is taken into account, 30% of tenants of furnished accommodation in 1979 paid more than 20% of their gross income in rent as compared to 14% of the total population; 16% paid more than 30% as compared to 4% overall (Table 12). As a result, the median rent/income proportion for furnished tenants was 16% compared with 9% overall. In the unfurnished sub-sector, however, proportions are slightly below average and in job-related accommodation very few pay high proportions. Thus hardship defined in this way is concentrated among furnished tenants who, as we have already seen, receive relatively little accommodation for their money. The majority of others paying more than 20% are households at an early stage in their mortgage who are purchasing an asset as well as housing services.

Evidence from the PRSS (Todd et al. 1982) suggests that the problem is concentrated among lower-income households and among those who have recently moved – but that it is not especially high in London, as is usually assumed. Londoners' higher incomes appear to compensate for higher rents so that the proportion paying over 20% of their income is similar to the national average.

5 ii) Although rents in the unfurnished sub-sector are low, there are still large numbers of tenants paying high proportions of their income for housing.

The median rent/income ratio in the unfurnished sub-sector is slightly lower than the national average. However, the proportions paying above 25% of their income, after allowances, are similar to the average (Table 13). This represents significant hardship because these households consist mainly of those on the lowest incomes in the sub-sector. Moreover, median income in that sector is only just over half the national average. The *absolute* amount of income available for non-housing expenditure is therefore far less than in other tenures.

5 iii) Take-up of benefits is limited, particularly among tenants of furnished accommodation.

The figures on post-allowance rent/income ratios imply that there are large numbers of private tenants who are not receiving available housing assistance. Specific information on take-up is limited. The third, and final, Report of the Advisory Committee on Rent Rebates and Allowances suggested that take-up was limited to fewer than two-thirds of tenants of unfurnished accommodation and to a negligible proportion of those in

TABLE 13

Weekly mortgage/rent as % of usual gross weekly income of head of household and wife by selected tenures

Great Britain 1979

Percentage	Private Rented			All tenures (%)
	With job/business (%)	Unfurnished (%)	Furnished (%)	
Nil	65	11	11	5
Over 0 but under 5%	18	31	5	20
Over 5% but under 10%	12	25	18	32
Over 10% but under 15%	2	12	18	17
Over 15% but under 20%	1	10	18	12
Over 20% but under 25%	0	4	7	7
Over 25% but under 30%	0	3	7	3
30% or more	2	4	16	4
20% or more	2	11	30	14
(Base = 100%)	(238)	(691)	(238)	(7136)
Median	5	8	16	9

Source: General Household Survey 1979, Table 3.29 (b)

furnished accommodation (Department of Environment 1983b, para 2.18).

Thus even though income-related housing assistance has been available for more than a decade, there is still evidence of considerable hardship in the private rented sector. In the unfurnished part of the sector the majority of the problem arises from low incomes rather than high rents (although a significant proportion suffer both). In the furnished part the problem arises more from high rents, although many also have low incomes.

Equity between tenures

It has been generally accepted for many years that assistance given for housing purposes is tenure specific and has been a major cause of the decline of the PRS and of inequity between private renting and other tenures (Nevitt 1966; Department of Environment 1977a). This, together with constraints on access to the majority tenures, has meant not just that those remaining in private renting have received a poor deal but also that they are among the worst off in society. The effect of housing subsidies is therefore inequitable not just between tenures but also between different income groups. The other side of the coin is that non-neutral treatment of tenures results in additional incentives to landlords to invest elsewhere and to reduce their involvement in private renting, making conditions in the sector even worse.

Detailed hypotheses include:

6 i) Tenure choice is distorted by subsidies, leaving private tenants particularly badly off.

While there is no general agreement about what represents a subsidy, all commentators are agreed that private tenants receive no general assistance from government sources (Ermisch 1984) and as we have already shown, income-related benefits are less effective than elsewhere.

In the majority tenures, most if not all households receive

assistance, either in the form of tax reliefs (mortgage interest relief or the lack of tax on imputed income and on capital gains) in the owner-occupied sector, or by paying rents below market levels in the public sector (Ermisch 1984; Grey et al. 1981). The extent of subsidy involved is very considerable, even though the value of the benefit has recently been declining sharply in the public sector (Ermisch 1984): indeed, in a few areas, public sector rents may now be above equilibrium market levels. In the private rented sector those whose rents are regulated at a rent below the market rent receive assistance – but this comes mostly from the landlord rather than the government[6] and brings with it the incentive to the landlord to avoid regulation, or to leave the sector, with adverse consequences for many tenants.

With respect to housing benefit, the conditions of eligibility for private tenants are similar to those found in the public sector, so in this sense they are not disadvantaged. However, take-up of benefit among private tenants is far less than among public tenants (Department of Environment 1983b), in part because the agency responsible for paying the benefit is also usually the public sector landlord, in part because circumstances in the PRS change more often, and in part because of lack of knowledge by private tenants about the system. Thus all aspects of present housing subsidies clearly disadvantage private tenants in comparison to households in other tenures.

6 ii) Those in the PRS pay more for equivalent
       accommodation than in other tenures.

In the unregulated part of the sector, there is an implication that private tenants paying market rents will pay more per unit of accommodation than those in the public sector where rents are not market determined. In the regulated part the position depends on the extent and effectiveness of rent control.

Family Expenditure Survey data suggest that furnished tenants pay about 10% more than the average for all tenures for their accommodation (Table 11). We have already seen that more than half of those who share live in that sub-sector (Table 6), and that although household size is far smaller than average, the proportion overcrowded is highest (Table 11), and the proportion with more than two rooms per person is least (Table 12). These factors suggest that indeed furnished tenants pay more per unit for their accommodation than households in other tenures.

On average, tenants of unfurnished accommodation pay 75% of that paid by all households, and 86% of that paid by public tenants (Table 11). They have a low propensity to share facilities or accommodation, their overcrowding levels are comparable to owner-occupation and 70% have more than two rooms per person. In quantity terms therefore they do somewhat better than other tenures. Even here, the majority are small households so owner-occupiers in particular receive absolutely more accommodation per household member for their money. Moreover, in London, as we have seen, private unfurnished tenants of one-bedroom accommodation paid 23% more than council tenants of similar accommodation. Where unfurnished tenants undoubtedly do suffer is in the quality of accommodation they receive. Dwellings are more likely to be older, to be unfit, and to require significant repair than elsewhere in the housing stock, and only about one in five have central heating (O.P.C.S. 1983a, Table 3.36). It would need more detailed analysis than is possible here to determine whether the extent of poor quality more than offsets the low rents paid – but for many tenants this is likely to be the case.

Overall, therefore, it would appear that private tenants do badly both in terms of direct subsidy and in terms of value for money.

6 iii) Private tenants have lower incomes on average so the overall effects of housing subsidies and controls are regressive.

We have already shown in 2 (ii) above that private tenants, except those in job-related employment, have lower than average incomes not just in terms of the median but throughout the relative income ranges. Moreover, it is not simply a result of a different mix of households in the different sectors – it is, for instance, true both for those who are economically active and for those who are not. The position is so poor for tenants of unfurnished accommodation that it undoubtedly offsets any relative benefit of rent control. Among tenants of furnished accommodation it exacerbates the already bad position arising from market rents and poor value for money. It is therefore clear that indeed the effect of housing subsidies is regressive.

6 iv) There is little incentive to remain or invest in the sector.

Evidence to the Select Committee on Environment suggested that in many areas the price obtainable on tenanted property could be only 25–33% of that sold with vacant possession (House of Commons Environment Committee 1982a, para 38). This is a capitalised reflection of the difference between the expected rental income and the value of the property elsewhere – usually in owner-occupation. It is thus the imputed cost of investing in property let on a regulated tenancy.

The second piece of evidence is the continuing decline of the sector at a rate of perhaps 100,000 dwellings per year. This should be understood alongside survey material which shows that most landlords, at least of potentially regulated tenancies, have no intention to relet once they obtain full vacant possession of their property (Whitehead 1978).

Thirdly, there is evidence that private landlords are not generally prepared to put additional investment into their property through improvement and repair. We have already seen that unfitness and the need for large-scale repair is concentrated in the sector (Table 3).

There is, however, some very limited evidence of a change in behaviour in this respect. A study of four areas in the North West (Martin 1985) has shown an intention on the part of some landlords to invest and remain in the sector, at least for a while, where there are large-scale subsidies and lettings do not provide security of tenure. This suggests that within a market environment there is some level of assistance which would induce investment, at least in the existing stock. However, this is not a general finding in relationship to current conditions.

Lastly, there is some evidence of continuing supply of accommodation by resident landlords. A survey by OPCS of recent lettings to households in the private rented sector in 1982-4 found that 5% of such lettings were by resident landlords. This suggests that there may have been up to 12,500 new lettings per annum in the early 1980s by resident landlords. Moreover, the change in the OPCS definition of "separate household" after 1981 means that those tenants of resident landlords who share a living room with the landlord will not have been included. If such households are included, the total may be as high as 46,000 (Todd 1986). This can be compared with the estimate from the 1977 NDHS follow-up survey of 47,000 new lettings by resident landlords (Todd et al 1982, Table 3.2), implying roughly a "steady state" in this sub-sector, with sources of new supply balancing those leaving the sector.

Overall, the evidence suggests that conditions in the sector relative to those available elsewhere are poor for most tenants, whether secure or not, and for most landlords (at least of regulated tenancies). Moreover, many of the tenants affected are among the poorest households in the country. Conditions are therefore clearly inequitable both vertically, between income groups, and horizontally, between private renting and other tenures.

Access to the sector

The lack of incentive to supply on the part of most landlords and of ability to pay on the part of many tenants and potential tenants implies that there are likely to be significant problems of access to the sector. This we have suggested means that conditions are not just inadequate for many of those already there but also make it more difficult for those trying to enter the housing market to find anything at all. Detailed hypotheses therefore include:

7 i)   There are many concealed households who are unable to obtain accommodation.

The NDHS found that in England in 1976 there were some 253,000 families or married couple households living within another household (Department of Environment 1979). Evidence from the Census suggests a figure of 317,000 concealed households in 1981 (Department of Environment 1985a, p. 7). While these two figures are not strictly comparable, this does at the very least suggest there has been little or no reduction in the numbers of concealed households in the period 1976–1981, and probably that there has been a significant increase among single parent households. Moreover, the problem is heavily concentrated in central urban areas.

Some of these households may not wish to live separately; a Department of Environment survey suggested that nearly 60% in fact wanted to live with others (Rauta, 1986). However, there clearly remains a problem, which is not significantly declining, of households unable to meet their housing needs either through the market or via socially provided housing.

7 ii)   Many potential tenants have to live in bed-and-breakfast and hostel accommodation.

In 1984 there were some 139,000 people in receipt of Supplementary Benefit who were living in bed-and-breakfast, lodging house or hostel accommodation. This represents an increase of 150% from 1980 (Conway and Kemp 1985, p. 15). Many observers believe that these numbers are increasing rapidly, especially in London.[7] It is thus clear that there is a shortage of accommodation and difficulties of access to housing at least at rents which the DHSS is prepared to pay through housing benefit.

7 iii) A significant proportion of homeless families have never managed to obtain accommodation in the housing market.

Evidence on homeless families accepted by local authorities shows that nearly 40% of those accepted had been living with family or friends and a further 13% did not come from the three main tenures (although an unknown proportion of these will have been previously living in one of the three tenures at an earlier stage of their housing history) (*Housing and Construction Statistics*, June 1980, Table 2.27). More detailed information from a study in London which used a wider definition of homelessness also suggested that more than one-third of homeless households had never found separate accommodation. Moreover, the proportion of homeless households who had come from the private rented sector fell from 51% in 1972 to 32% in 1981 (Austerberry, Schott and Watson 1984, Table 5.4).

Thus there is evidence that even with the availability of income-related housing benefits, there are significant numbers of people who are unable to find accommodation. Conditions of access in the private rented sector are therefore shown to be inadequate. It should, however, be remembered that there are still large numbers of new lets taking place in the private rented sector (although the numbers appear to have declined from over half a million in 1976 [Department of Environment 1979] to less than 300,000 in 1981 [O.P.C.S. 1983c]), and that these account for almost one quarter of all moves.

1. The 1983/4 GLC Survey came to very similar conclusions with regard to London (GLC 1985).

2. The PRSS (Todd et al 1982) for instance found a strong relationship between date of letting and the proportion of households living at two or more above bedroom standard.

3. Even within this group there may be rents below market clearing levels because many landlords let for non-market reasons, e.g. to friends and relatives.

4. The differential is not so great in the furnished sub-sector because 'recent lettings' comprise 76% of all lettings.

5. This comparison is becoming less clear-cut as public sector rents rise more rapidly than registered rents in the private sector.

6. Though see footnote 9, p. 20.

7. Moreover, in 1985 the Government sought to restrict the ability of young persons to obtain such accommodation through changes in the regulations governing the required supplementary benefits payments. This move was prompted partly because of the huge increase in the number of such payments that were being made.

Chapter 3   The role of the private rented sector in the
            housing market

The demand for private renting

The three areas where consumer choice may lead to private
renting that we have identified relate to the provision of (i) easy
access accommodation, (ii) housing for long-term tenants and for
non-traditional households, and (iii) job-related accommodation.
Evidence that the sector fulfils these roles does not necessarily
show that people are obtaining what they want, although it may
suggest that the role is necessary, at least given current conditions.
To examine this dichotomy we look at evidence on satisfaction
before turning to evidence on the extent to which private renting is
still the tenure of last resort.

The first group of detailed hypotheses therefore relate to the
easy access role.

8 i) Newly forming households, especially those who are not
      married or have no children, initially enter the private
      rented sector.

The main evidence on the behaviour of newly-formed
households comes from the follow-up survey to the 1976 National
Household and Dwelling Survey, 'Recently Moving Households'
(O.P.C.S. 1983b). The 1981 Labour Force Survey also includes
some material.

In the 1977 survey half of all newly forming households went
into private renting (Table 14). As in the main survey only 16% of

58

TABLE 14

New households: marital status and household type by tenure

England 1977

	Owner occupied	Thousands (percentages) Public sector	PRS	Total
All new households	150	62	210	422
	(36%)	(15%)	(50%)	
Married	111	34	79	224
	(50%)	(15%)	(35%)	
Not married	39	28	131	198
	(20%)	(14%)	(66%)	
Single person aged 16–59	26	11	79	116
	(22%)	(9%)	(68%)	
Small adult household	91	12	73	176
	(52%)	(7%)	(41%)	
Small family	21	30	24	75
	(28%)	(40%)	(32%)	
Large family	1	2	2	5
	(20%)	(40%)	(40%)	
Large adult household	6	2	26	34
	(18%)	(6%)	(76%)	
Other small household	1	–		1
	(100%)			
Single person aged 60+	3	6	7	16
	(19%)	(38%)	(44%)	

Source: 'Recently Moving Households', Tables 2.3 and 3.4

all households were private tenants, this confirms the importance of the sector as the tenure by which people enter the housing market.

Over 60% of these households were unmarried as compared to 47% of all newly forming households. Family households were more likely to go into the local authority sector, while married couples without children usually became owner-occupiers. Private renting was thus concentrated among working-age single people, who accounted for 27% of all new households, and among large adult households who were presumably mainly groups of young people but accounted for only 8% of all new households. Our own calculations, based on 1981 Labour Force Survey data, found considerably fewer new households going into the PRS however.[1] Only 13% of new family households, and 34% of new non-family households, were private tenants, giving an overall figure of 29% for all new households. As with the NDHS, families were associated with the local authority sector and childless couples with owner-occupation. Thus, although the PRS continues to play an important role for newly formed households, which does not appear to have declined significantly between 1971 and 1978 (both the National Movers Survey of 1971 and the NDHS follow-up survey of 1978 show about one-third of married couple new households and two-thirds of other new households making their first home in the PRS), it appears that this role is declining significantly in the 1980s. While the LFS evidence may overstate this decline somewhat, it is broadly consistent with other evidence about the reduction of new lettings between 1976 and 1981.

8 ii) A large proportion of households who move long distances, or for reasons related to their job, move into the private rented sector.

In 1977 among existing households nearly 40% of those who moved for job reasons and nearly one-third of those who moved more than 50 miles moved into private rented accommodation. This compared with 31% of all moving households who went into the private rented sector (O.P.C.S. 1983b). Thus, although there is a slightly higher chance of using the private rented sector for job-related and longer moves, the differential is not as great as is usually thought. Undoubtedly owner-occupation is the normal tenure for such moves, in part because they are more likely to be made by higher-income households. The only group of movers for whom private renting remains predominant are households coming from abroad of whom 63% went into the PRS (O.P.C.S. 1983c, Table 6A).

Looking at the question another way, the proportion of economically active movers who went into private renting in 1981, at 23%, was exactly the same as the proportion of inactive movers (O.P.C.S. 1983c, Table 6A). Moreover, the proportion of those actually in work was also 23%. There is thus no evidence to uphold the view that private renting is particularly used by those seeking employment. These two sources taken together also suggest that the importance of private renting as the tenure for mobile households has been declining rapidly over the last few years – apparently by over a quarter in four years. Overall, these figures suggest that, given current constraints on the availability of private renting, the sector is not playing as great a part in the provision of easy access accommodation for existing households as might be expected, given the attributes of the tenure.

8 iii) Tenants in the furnished sub-sector move more often than others.

Again, the main evidence comes from the 1977 survey on recently moving households which shows that almost one-fifth of tenants in the furnished sub-sector moved in the previous year, as against about one in twenty of those in other tenures (O.P.C.S. 1983b). This certainly suggests that the furnished sub-sector caters for the mobile, although to what extent this involvement is a matter of choice cannot be directly determined.

One rather surprising finding, however, is the extent to which there is still significant movement into and within the unfurnished sub-sector. In the 1977 survey, 12% of all moves were into the unfurnished sub-sector while 4% of tenants of unfurnished accommodation had moved within that sub-sector (O.P.C.S. 1983b). This appears to be in direct contradiction to the generally held view that there are hardly any new lettings of unfurnished accommodation, but the survey does include Housing Associations as well as more traditional private landlords. Thus, while it is true both that moving households have a higher relative probability of moving into the furnished sub-sector (although absolutely it is still very much the minority) and that those in the furnished sub-sector have a very high propensity to move, it is untrue that there is a particularly low propensity to move into the unfurnished sub-sector. However, it seems likely that a much higher proportion of unfurnished lettings never really enter the market at all. For example, GLC data show that while 57% of tenants of recent furnished lettings in London in 1983/4 found the accommodation via an agency or advertisement, among recent unfurnished lettings the proportion fell to only 18%, the implication being that a much higher proportion of unfurnished lettings are through family and business connections or via informal networks.

8 iv) Those who suffer sudden changes in their circumstances find their housing in the private rented sector.

The only group which can readily be identified as changing their circumstances are those who have been divorced. Such households have a higher than average propensity (18%) to be in the PRS: this is particularly true of male divorced household heads (23%) (O.P.C.S. 1983d, Table 15). The figures may well be higher for those who have recently been divorced, but there are no data on this. The above evidence offers some support to the hypothesis, though one cannot rule out the possibility that 'divorced' status is correlated with another characteristic (such as social class) which itself is correlated with tenure. The differential between male and female percentages in the PRS among the divorced probably relates to the greater proportions of female partners remaining in the marital home.

All these figures suggest that a part of the private rented sector does indeed provide for newly forming mobile households. However, the concentration is not as great as might be expected and is not great enough to uphold the view that private renting is the main source of such accommodation.

The other aspect of the 'easy access' role is that those who are unable to obtain suitable accommodation elsewhere can be expected to find themselves in the private rented sector.

8 v) Many households that might not be expected to wish to rent privately are still found entering the sector.

26% of households moving into or within the sector in 1977 were families, whom one would not normally expect to regard private renting the best tenure for their needs (Table 15). This number includes those moving into Housing Association accommodation which is particularly suited to families, but is also likely to include many who are moving into insecure, poor quality units.

On the other hand, 60% of entrants were single people of working age or small adult households for whom private renting may be quite suitable. Only when one examines these findings in relation to preferences can one begin to see whether these findings are a function of choice or constraint (see 11 below).

One last point is that, perhaps surprisingly, there is no evidence that family households are more predominant in the private rented sector in areas of housing stress. While family households make up one in five of all households in the sector nationally, this proportion actually falls in stress areas to about one in seven (Table 16).

TABLE 15

Households moving into PRS* by household type

England 1977

	Thousands	%
Single person aged 16–59	173	31
Small adult household	157	29
Small family household	110	20
Large family household	32	6
Large adult household	49	9
Older, small household	10	2
Single person aged 60+	19	3
ALL HOUSEHOLD TYPES	550	100

* i.e. includes both new and continuing households
Source: 'Recently Moving Households', Table 3.3

TABLE 16

Private renting and household type:
Stress areas and all England compared

(a) Household type by tenure: percentage of households of each type found in the PRS

	'Stress' area %	All England %
Family households	7.9	7.0
Non-family households	19.5	13.2
All households	16.1	11.1

(b) Tenure by household type: breakdown of PRS into family and non-family households

	'Stress' areas %	All England %
Family households	14.3	20.9
Non-family households	85.5	79.0
All households	100.0	100.0

N.B.   'Stress' areas are the 49 Local Authority districts which show the greatest imbalance of households and dwellings, per 1000 households, according to the DoE's General Needs Indicator for household/dwelling balance.
Source: derived from Census Small Area Statistics 1981

The second role of the private rented sector is the provision of accommodation for long-term tenants and for non-traditional households. Specific hypotheses include:

9 i)   Many tenants, especially among pensioner households, have lived in the same private rented accommodation for many years.

Over one-third of private tenants in 1978 had been in their accommodation for more than ten years (Table 17). These were concentrated among pensioner households, of whom nearly 70% had lived there that long. Under 20% of other non-family households had lived in their accommodation for more than ten years, but this is more than double the number who had been there for between six and ten years – a different pattern than that found among family households where there were fairly similar

TABLE 17

Private renting households:
household type by when letting commenced

England 1978

Thousands (percentages)

	> 10 years ago	Letting commenced 6–10 years	< 6 years	All
Pensioner households	462	85	128	675
	(68%)	(13%)	(19%)	(100%)
Other non-family households	194	88	714	996
	(19%)	(9%)	(72%)	(100%)
Family households	60	53	248	361
	(17%)	(15%)	(69%)	(100%)
Not known	1	–	2	3
ALL	717	226	1092	2033
	(35%)	(11%)	(54%)	(100%)

Source: Todd et al., The Privately Rented Sector in 1978, Table 4.15

proportions in the two groups. This does suggest that there is a small but significant proportion of non-pensioner households who find their long-term home in the sector. On the other hand, the vast majority of non-pensioner households had lived in their accommodation for less than six years. The data thus reflect the two quite different roles played by the sector.

9 ii) Single people and other non-traditional households are more likely to be housed in the private rented sector than in the majority tenures.

25% of single adults of working age live in the private rented sector, as do 18% of households made up of three or more adults (O.P.C.S. 1983d). While these figures imply some concentration of such households in the sector, they also show that the vast majority of such households live elsewhere. Indeed, overall only 14% of non-family households live in the sector, as compared to 11% of households overall (O.P.C.S. 1983d). The extent of concentration is hence nothing like as great as many assume.

Thus the evidence suggests that the private rented sector does play an important and disproportionate role in the long-term provision of housing for the elderly (many of whom have always lived in the sector) and to a lesser extent for younger non-family households, this second role being most important among the single. However, the majority of even these households live in the main tenures and most of those currently in private renting will, on past experience, move on to other tenures.

The final role is that of job-related accommodation. Here one would expect to find households mainly because of their jobs rather than because of their housing needs. There may, however, be others who take the job because of the accommodation.

10 i) Households in the job-related sub-sector will be similar to other working households.

The proportion of married couples with children is far higher in the job-related sub-sector than for households overall (Table 7), as is to a lesser extent the proportion of married couples without children.

10 ii) A high proportion of households in the sub-sector works in agriculture, the armed forces, the police and in locationally specific services.

Analysis of data from the 1981 Labour Force Survey shows that 18.5% of households in Britain in job-related private rented housing are agricultural workers. A further 9.1% are members of the armed forces. So, over a quarter of the sub-sector is found in these two occupational categories. This means that more than half of all agricultural workers, and over one-third of forces employees are in job-related private rented accommodation.

10 iii) Average incomes in the sub-sector are lower than for other working households.

The rationale behind this fairly generally held view is twofold:

(a) such households have lower housing costs so can expect lower incomes (others, especially agricultural workers, may get some income in kind), and
(b) if they had to take the job because of lack of housing they would be in a poor bargaining position.

In fact, the evidence suggests that mean and median incomes are higher than for all households (Table 8). This remains true if we compare only economically active households. This suggests that there is no direct evidence of financial pressure forcing the choice of such accommodation.

As far as demand for private renting is concerned, therefore, the overall picture is much as predicted – with clear evidence of the three roles hypothesised above (p. 58). But in addition there is still some evidence of households entering the sector who might be expected to be far better served elsewhere. The only way to distinguish within each of these groups between those who are reasonably happy with their choice of tenure and those who feel that they have no real choice is to examine the extent to which such households are satisfied with their accommodation and their preferences with respect to tenure. What one would expect to find is that private tenants are generally less happy with their accommodation but that satisfaction will vary between different household types. Similarly, one would expect preference for private renting to be very limited but greater than average among those for whom the tenure might be expected to be more suitable, on *a priori* grounds. Detailed hypotheses include:

11 ii) There is a relatively high level of dissatisfaction with private renting.

The level of satisfaction in the furnished rented sub-sector is generally lower than elsewhere. Its mean 'satisfaction score' in the General Household Survey in 1978 for instance was 3.8 as against

4.3 overall. The score for the unfurnished sub-sector at 4.0 was, however, no lower than that for the local authority sector – although the proportion that was very dissatisfied was slightly higher (Table 18). Overall, 19% of tenants of both furnished and unfurnished accommodation were dissatisfied as against 11% of all households.

Among those renting with job and business the average score was 4.2, close to the overall average; the proportions positively dissatisfied were also similar.

Thus the average levels of dissatisfaction are not as low as perhaps might be expected, but nearly one in five of non-employee private tenants are dissatisfied with what they receive. What is more surprising is that this dissatisfaction is not especially concentrated among tenants of furnished accommodation where conditions are more difficult.

11 ii) Satisfaction is concentrated among long-term tenants and the young and mobile who state a preference for private renting.

There is very little evidence which distinguishes by tenure and household type. The "Attitudes to Letting" Survey in 1976 asked private tenants whether they preferred private renting to other tenures. This showed that 45% of elderly tenants preferred the private rented sector while this proportion fell to 17% among families and large adult households, and to 16% among small adult households (Paley 1978).

11 iii)Preference for private renting is concentrated among the elderly and among young adults – the first because they have always been in the sector and the second because the attributes of private renting are most suitable for this group.

As has been seen above, in 1976, 45% of elderly tenants preferred private renting. This was consistent with the Building Societies Association Survey in 1983 which showed 50% of those already in

TABLE 18

Satisfaction with accommodation by tenure and household type

Tenure	Level of satisfaction					Base =100%	Mean score
	Very satisfied %	Fairly satisfied %	Neither satisfied nor dissatisfied %	A little dissatisfied %	Very dissatisfied %		
	Score:5	4	3	2	1		
Owner-occupied owned outright	72	22	2	3	2	2528	4.6
Owner-occupied with mortgage	56	36	2	5	1	3317	4.4
Rented with job/business	50	35	4	7	4	312	4.2
Rented from LA or NT	43	37	4	9	7	3823	4.0
Rented from HA or co-operative	50	31	3	8	9	117	4.1
Rented privately – unfurnished	44	33	5	10	9	816	4.0
Rented privately – furnished	28	43	9	10	9	269	3.8
ALL HOUSEHOLDS	53	33	3	7	4	11206	4.3

Source: General Household Survey 1978, Table 4.1

the unfurnished sub-sector wanted to be in that tenure in two years' time (Table 19). On the other hand, only 14% of those in furnished accommodation wanted to be in that sector in two years' time. This in part reflects the fact that few people want to be tenants for long.

The 16–19 year-old age group had the highest preference for private renting. Even so, only 9% wanted to rent private furnished accommodation and a further 6% wanted a private unfurnished unit (Table 19).

11 iv) Few non-pensioner households wish to rent in the longer term.

The material from the BSA survey, which showed only 4% of respondents wanting to rent privately in two years' time, certainly confirms this view (Building Societies Association 1983). Among those already in the sector, the proportions would clearly be higher – but, except for the elderly, would still be very low. Even among those renting with job and business, only 25% positively wanted to rent in two years' time. Most younger households clearly prefer owner-occupation.

Overall, therefore, the evidence suggests that although the private rented sector is providing a range of accommodation for different types of people, the vast majority would prefer another tenure. Only among the elderly long-term tenants is there a significant continuing preference for private renting. These preferences do not take account of relative costs, so they do not imply that there is no demand, but rather that if they had a free choice people would choose other than private renting.

The operation of the supply side

So far we have looked at the way the operation of the private rented sector affects households in that sector and those trying to become private tenants. But whether there are problems in the sector depends as much on supply as on demand. In particular, in

TABLE 19

Accommodation most like to be living in, in two years time by age, marital status and present tenure

	All	Age				Marital status		Present tenure:		
		16–19	20–24	25–64	65+	Married	Single	PRS furn.	PRS unf.	PRS bus/emp.
Owned	77	73	84	83	56	82	65	76	44	54
Rented from Council	16	10	7	14	33	14	21	5	5	–
Rented private: furnished	1	9	5	–	–	–	4	14	–	9
Rented private: unfurnished	3	6	3	2	8	2	7	3	50	16
Don't know	2	3	1	2	3	1	3	2	1	21
TOTAL	100	100	100	100	100	100	100	100	100	100
Sample size (N)	2499	204	246	1555	495	1721	778	39	126	35

Source: Building Societies Association (1983)

a sector in decline a major source of stress arises if the rate of decline of supply is greater than that of demand. We therefore now turn to an examination of hypotheses about the way the supply side of the private rented sector operates.

The general wisdom suggests that private landlords either are rapacious, operating outside the constraints of the Rent Acts, or obtain a bad deal from renting and have little incentive to re-let. We look first at the traditional part of the sector where the majority of lettings in the past has been made within the framework of the security and rent control legislation.

12 i) The number of lettings by traditional landlords is in continuous decline.

The number of households and dwellings in the private sector overall has been in continuous decline since at least 1938. At that time there were over six million privately rented units in England (57% of the stock). By the late 1970s the number of units had fallen to about two million (less than 12% of the total stock) (House of Commons Environment Committee 1982a, Chapter 2). In the 1980s the decline has continued: the private rented sector in December 1984 was estimated at 1.7 million units (9% of the total) (Department of Environment 1985c).

The fastest rate of decline has been in the traditional unfurnished sub-sector – which fell from 12% of households in Great Britain in 1971 to 6% in 1982 (O.P.C.S. 1983a, 1984). The share of furnished accommodation within the PRS on the other hand has increased at least since 1966 (although continuing to fall in absolute terms) and the share of tied accommodation has also increased during the 1970s (O.P.C.S. 1983a, 1984). These data suggest that indeed decline has been concentrated in the traditional part of the sector.

It is more difficult to assess national trends in terms of type of landlord. In London at the time of the Milner Holland Report 30% of dwellings were provided by property companies (Milner Holland 1965). By the time of the PRSS survey in 1978 that proportion had fallen to 21% (Todd et al. 1982). At the time of their inquiry into the private rented sector, which reported in 1982, the House of Commons Select Committee was unable to find evidence of any large property company that was increasing its holding or even keeping it stable. They concluded that "on the basis of the evidence presented . . . those landlords whose main objective was long-term investment, that is, companies and non-resident individual landlords, were likely to continue to reduce their investment in the sector" (House of Commons Environment Committee 1982a, para 26).

Lastly, contrary to much received opinion, there is no evidence of any increase in the supply of accommodation by resident landlords. It is sometimes argued that the nature of such lettings renders them especially liable to under-estimation in censuses and surveys. Even using our generous estimates from the O.P.C.S. 1982–4 survey referred to above (p. 54) produces a figure for the early 1980s which is no larger than that for the mid-1970s. Of course, if the numbers of new lettings by resident landlords remain fairly constant, or at least decline more slowly than other parts of the sector, they will of course come to represent an increasing proportion of lettings in relative terms.

12 ii) There is a significant difference between the capital value of tenanted property and similar units sold with vacant possession.

The difference between the value of a vacant property and that same property with a tenant is one measure of the incentive to sell facing landlords of such property when they obtain vacant possession (Doling and Davies 1984). It therefore reflects the extent to which security of tenure and rent control limit the landlord's capacity to use his/her asset in the most profitable way. The extent of this difference between tenanted and vacant possession values will vary in relation to the local pressures in the housing market. Where the owner-occupied market is buoyant and fair rents exclude a significant scarcity element, the difference can be very large; in more depressed areas rents may be far more closely related to market values and the differences could be quite small.

The majority of evidence on the extent of such differences relates to individual instances or the general impressions of estate agents and others operating in the field. The best source is again the Select Committee Report which stated that:

> "A wide range of respondents gave evidence [to the Committee] on the extent of this difference in capital values. Estimates suggested that tenanted property could sell for as little as 20% of its vacant possession value, although on average it probably sold for between one third and one half."
> (House of Commons Environment Committee 1982a, para 38).

The sources of these estimates included not only the two main landlord associations but also local authorities and a wide range of individuals. There thus seems no doubt that in most areas landlords currently letting within the Rent Acts who gain vacant possession have little economic incentive to relet, at least within the current legislative framework.

The next hypothesis follows from this conclusion:

12 iii) There are few relets by landlords under the Rent Act conditions.

The National Dwelling and Housing Survey (NDHS) in 1977 found that there had been about 500,000 new lettings in England in the previous year (Department of Environment 1979). By the time of the 1981 Census this number appeared to have fallen to under 300,000 (O.P.C.S. 1983c, Table 6A).

The status of these lettings cannot readily be determined without detailed knowledge about the exact nature of the agreements. The Department of Environment indicated that perhaps 80% of the new lettings in the NDHS were regulated tenancies (House of Commons Environment Committee 1982c, p. 25) – but this total includes the lettings that could not formally be excluded on the available information. The 1983/84 GLC survey, a major aim of which was to clarify the extent to which lettings were outside the Rent Act, found that while 66% of all tenancies in the survey were probably protected, less than a third of lettings made after 1980 were in that category (GLC 1986).

Moreover, questions on tenants' perceptions of their legal status suggested that only just over one-third of all tenants understood that they were protected. This implies that a high proportion of agreements if contested might turn out to be within the Rent Acts but that the tenant, and quite possibly the landlord, is unaware of the level of protection provided. Other surveys have come to similar conclusions (Pearce 1982, Todd 1986). In addition, there was evidence that lettings outside the Rent Acts were concentrated in Central London where demand was highest (GLC 1985, 1986).

Thus the statistical evidence suggests that new lettings are much less likely to be subject to the Rent Acts than longer-term tenancies, but that many of such lettings are not formally excluded from protection. Even this conclusion is inconsistent with the advice given to landlords by their associations. In their evidence to the Environment Committee, the Small Landlords Association said, for instance, that their advice to any landlord contemplating a new let would be "avoid at all costs creating a fully protected tenancy"; while the British Property Federation argues that "there is no reason at all why anyone should structure his affairs in such a way that he gives more security of tenure . . . or anything else than he has to". Additionally, other witnesses argued that in some parts of the country, particularly Central London, virtually all new lettings were outside the Rent Act (House of Commons Environment Committee 1982a, para 23).

The evidence led the Committee to conclude that:

"Information submitted to the Committee regarding such lettings [i.e. those outside the Rent Act] was neither statistically nor legally comprehensive in its coverage. However, it was of sufficient volume and quality for the conclusion to be drawn that in certain areas, especially in Inner London, such lettings form a significant proportion of available vacant accommodation."

(House of Commons Environment Committee 1982a, para 89).

Thus, although the hypothesis that 'no one' relets within the Rent Acts is an overstatement, the extent of formal protection among new lettings is clearly limited and the extent to which landlords and tenants perceive that protection is even less. Moreover, the proportion of protected tenancies is probably correlated with the 'tightness' of the housing market – in stress areas, where rates of return on unregulated tenancies can be very high, the extent of protection is less.

The second related hypothesis is that:

12 iv) New lets will be concentrated in property which is unsuitable for home ownership and therefore has a relatively low sale value on the owner-occupied market.

In the NDHS follow-up survey on recently moving households, over 40% of lettings were of converted flats and rooms. Yet well over one-third were of whole houses and a further 19% of purpose-built flats (O.P.C.S. 1983b). This suggests that the majority of new lettings are still of property that has a possible alternative use. Of course, this figure includes lettings by housing associations, employers and absentee owner-occupiers, as well as lettings of poor quality units and dwellings in areas where there is low demand for owner-occupation. However, there is evidence of some reletting of property which would be unexpected on economic grounds.

On the other hand, the PRSS found that nearly two-fifths of new lettings were of accommodation in which rooms or amenities are shared, as compared to about 5% of lettings made in 1961 or before. Our own analysis of data from the Labour Force Survey found that in Britain in 1981, 23.3% of lettings[2] made within the previous two years involved households having to share rooms, compared with only 12.0% for the sector as a whole.

The final related hypothesis, is that:

12 v) Most traditional landlords only let because of the security legislation and would rather sell up if they could obtain vacant possession prices.

The last detailed study of landlord intentions was the Attitudes to Letting Survey in 1976 (Paley 1978). This found that among companies and non-residential individual landlords fewer than 40% intended to relet their accommodation if they obtained vacant possession of the whole building. If, however, only the unit, as opposed to the building, was vacant over 50% would relet.

This evidence suggests, first, that vacant possession is a major factor determining landlords' decisions and thus that security of tenure restricts their choices. Second, it suggests that the majority of traditional landlords will leave the sector when given the opportunity but that a significant minority relet. Of course, there is no evidence about the terms under which such lettings would be made.

Overall, the evidence on landlord behaviour points to continuing decline in the sector and the replacement, when new lettings occur, of old-style protected tenancies by lettings formally or informally outside the Rent Acts providing smaller, often shared accommodation. However, the evidence does not suggest that all existing landlords, even non-resident individuals and company landlords who could be expected to let for profit-making reasons, follow this pattern. There is evidence of reletting under the Rent Acts even of property that has the potential for owner-occupation. The data on the overall number of new lets suggest, however, that the decline of the sector is certainly continuing, and perhaps even accelerating slightly between 1977 and 1981.

The second group of hypotheses about the supply side relates to the rents that landlords are able to obtain when they let. Only if the rate of return that can be obtained on rental alone is adequate in comparison to the return available on investing those funds elsewhere will a landlord letting for financial reasons be prepared to relet. The calculation is complicated and is made up not just of the expected rent but also of the expectations of future capital gains and of returns elsewhere (House of Commons Environment Committee 1982a, paras 40–44). It will be heavily dependent upon individual circumstances, but on average if rents do not in themselves provide roughly the same return as is available on relatively low-risk investments there will be an incentive to landlords to continue to leave the sector.

Thus the first detailed hypothesis is:

13 i) The average rate of return available on new lettings is below that necessary to keep the sector at its present size.

Given the many different factors involved, there can be no complete agreement about the required rate. However, in their evidence to the Environment Committee, "a number of respondents agreed with the view put forward by the British Property Federation that a rental return on vacant possession of 6% net (about 9% gross) would be necessary to maintain the supply of privately rented accommodation at its current level" (House of Commons 1982a, para 41). This assumes that inflation will be dealt with through commensurate increases in capital values.

The main source of information on rental rates of return is the Department of Environment's Beacons Survey which covers all types of regulated registered rent accommodation. Table 20 gives some of the results of the January 1985 survey. The Beacons Survey shows that rates vary between areas (especially between London and the rest of the country) and between types of property. There is only a slight inverse relationship between expected saleability of the property and the rate of return achieved, but there is a much stronger correlation between area and return. In areas where there is little pressure on the housing market, rates of return at least for the upper quartile and sometimes for the median tend towards that seen to be necessary

TABLE 20

Annual gross rates of return on capital values
of DOE "Beacon" properties

January 1985

Type of property	London		Rest of England & Wales		All England & Wales	
	Mean	Median	Mean	Median	Mean	Median
Beacon A	2.4	3	3.9	5	3.2	4
Beacon C	3.0	3	4.4	5	3.7	4
Beacon D	2.8	3	3.9	4	3.5	4
Beacon E	3.2	3	4.5	5	3.9	4

N.B.

Beacon A: unimproved, mid-terrace two-storey house built c1870.
Beacon C: larger mid-terrace two-storey house, built c1880 and improved to '10-point' standard.
Beacon D: two-storey semi-detached house, built mid-1930s.
Beacon E: self-contained purpose-built first-floor flat in 3 or more storey block built in early 1960s.

Source: DOE "Beacons" Exercise Return for 1.1.85

to keep the property in the sector. In areas of pressure, the rates of return are far below the opportunity cost if full capital value can be realised on sale with vacant possession.

Although the data do not distinguish between new and existing lettings, they do suggest that in the majority of cases registered rents are inadequate to maintain the current level of provision, particularly in areas of stress where a large proportion of the privately rented stock is located.

To the extent that new lettings are outside the Rent Acts, rents for such lettings can be expected to be significantly higher than in the registered sector. A relevant question is how much higher and therefore to what extent can letting outside the Rent Acts enable the current level of provision to be maintained.

The next hypothesis is, therefore:

13 ii) That rents, and therefore the rate of return, obtainable are negatively related to the extent of effective control.

The House of Commons Select Committee examined this point in some detail, and concluded that:

"Evidence on the level of unregistered rents obtained on regulated property was far more limited. What there was suggested that such rents were on average higher than in the registered sub-sector, by perhaps 20% overall and possibly 30% in London. Such rents might increase the gross rate of return on this type of property to between 3–6%. However, it should be noted that the variation around the mean was much greater, so that some landlords were probably making well over 10%." (House of Commons 1982a, para 35).

Indeed, individual examples were cited where unregulated rents were three or four times the fair rent on equivalent property.

Evidence from the 1978 Private Rented Sector Survey confirms this point. This showed that median unregistered rents were about 25% higher than median registered rents in England as a whole, and about one-third higher in London. Within this average, the 'unregistered' sub-sector contained some very low rents, probably for lettings to friends, relations or employees, and some very high rents. At the top end of the scale, unregistered rents were 50% above the highest registered lettings and in London the difference was 100%. Rents of accommodation where the landlord was resident were also considerably higher than registered rents, the median rent being asked by a resident landlord being 20% higher than median registered rents, and the highest rents in the resident landlord sub-sector being 50% greater than the highest registered rents (Todd et al. 1982). In real terms, these differences may be even higher as the average size of such lettings is much less and there is a much higher incidence of sharing.

Finally, as we have seen, the 1983/84 GLC survey found that the average rent per room in 'protected' tenancies was only £7.64, while that for 'unprotected' tenancies was £23.29. This ratio of nearly 1:3 can in part be attributed to location (unprotected tenancies are concentrated in the central areas), to furnishings, to length of time in the property, and to quality of the accommodation, but even if full adjustment were made for these factors a wide difference would remain (GLC 1985, para 40).

Yet, while the general picture shows higher rents where there is less regulation, there are some areas where the hypothesis does not hold. For instance, the Environment Committee found that "in a small number of areas fair rents are already thought to be at market levels" (House of Commons 1982a, para 42). In these areas it will presumably not be possible for landlords to increase rent levels, and hence their rates of return, by going outside the Rent Acts. This contrasts with the very strong evidence (reported by the Committee and by the GLC) of high rents for lettings outside the Rent Acts being concentrated in central urban areas, particularly Inner London.

Given that rents clearly relate both to the level of control and to the extent of demand pressure, what does this imply for the long-term level of provision in the sector? In particular:

13 iii) If all rents were raised to market levels, would the current size of the sector be viable?

If rent controls were to be removed and existing registered rents rose to the level of unregistered rents (i.e. by anything between zero and 30% depending on the type of property and the area), these rents would apparently still not generally provide the level of return necessary to keep landlords' investment in the sector at its current level (Whitehead and Kleinman 1986; Crook and Martin 1986). Areas where rates of return are high enough to provide 6–10% gross return on capital value are mainly areas of low demand for owner-occupation and general excess supply. As a result the current value return is based on values well below replacement cost. There is thus no incentive to invest in additional units and little to improve the property. The alternative will generally be low quality owner-occupation or vacancy. In these areas it will be demand that determines the extent of utilisation of the stock and the size of the private rented sector – and the evidence of the last decade is that the demand is continuing to decline (although see Chapter 4).

In parts of the market where high rents are available outside the Rent Acts, some landlords clearly do make good returns. While such lettings are the most buoyant part of the market, there is still evidence of continuing decline even in those sub-sectors where these lettings are concentrated (resident landlords, units in multi-occupation etc.). This implies that in current conditions this return is not adequate to stem the decline. It can be argued that this is not a true test of viability as present unregistered rents are not 'true' market rents because the level which is privately agreed is constrained downwards by the landlord's desire not to provoke the tenant into seeking a rent registration. However, this is offset by two other factors. First, tenants are often either ignorant of their rights in regard to the registration of rents, or believe, validly or otherwise, that the letting is outside the Rent Acts. Secondly, in the present situation where there is the possibility of Rent Act legislation being invoked by the tenant, the landlord's calculation of a sufficient rate of return may include a 'risk premium', so that some rents are actually higher than would be achieved in a free market.

Undoubtedly, if there were a completely free market the pattern of rents could be different and the average return required might be lower, because of reduced risk or landlords finding that the return they say they require is excessive. However, given the strength of decline in the past few years, it is difficult to imagine that required rents would not on average have to be higher than at present. In the unfurnished sub-sector, which accounts for two-thirds of all non-employer lettings, rents would have to rise very significantly for the decline in size to be halted. But this would run into two demand-side difficulties. First, as described above, private tenants, particularly unfurnished tenants, have relatively low incomes. Median household income in the unfurnished sub-sector is only 53% of all-households median income (Table 8), while almost a quarter of unfurnished tenants are already paying more than 20% of income in rent and rates. Hence it is difficult to see how the majority of tenants would be able to pay significantly higher rents.

Second, for those tenants who could afford to pay the required higher rents, it becomes a question not of ability but of preparedness to pay. Many tenants in this position would probably find it more desirable and cheaper to become owner-occupiers. In its evidence to the Environment Committee in 1981, SHAC, the London housing aid centre, gave an example of a landlord of a converted one-bedroom property who would have to charge £53.50 rent a week just to cover his costs, while the property could be bought on mortgage for £31 per week net (House of Commons Environment Committee 1982b, para 93).

All the evidence therefore suggests that there is not, in current circumstances, enough effective demand to keep suppliers in the market so that the sector remains at its current size. Whether or not this will continue to be the case in the future depends on many factors – which are discussed in the next chapter.

With respect to landlord behaviour we therefore conclude that:

The rate of return available for lettings made within the Rent Acts is generally well below the market rent and even where it is close to the market level there is little incentive to make additional or even replacement investment. This part of the sector must inevitably decline, and the speed of that decline will be determined mainly by the rate at which secure tenants vacate their accommodation. Yet even in the regulated part of the sector there is evidence of some reletting arising perhaps from inertia, from landlords wishing to let for non-economic reasons, or, in some cases, because there is no better alternative. However, evidence on the nature of new lettings suggests that on many occasions where regulated property is relet the type of letting will be changed to bring it formally or informally outside the Rent Acts.

Secondly, the evidence on new lettings suggests that the decline in the number made available would continue, even if average rents rose to the levels now found among non-Rent Act lettings. This arises both from the range of alternative investments available to landlords with vacant property and from the lack of effective demand on the part of tenants.

The extent of pressure

The final set of questions to examine in relation to the current situation is whether the rate of decline in supply is matched by that in demand – thus presenting few problems – or whether actual supply is inadequate to meet the demands made upon it – and particularly whether the sector is still able to maintain its role as the easy access sector.

The general hypothesis we put forward was that the private rented sector is indeed not fulfilling its role and that this results in considerable pressure in the rental market. Detailed hypotheses include:

14 i) Many homeless families are unable to find private rented accommodation.

The main source of information here is evidence of households accepted as homeless by local authorities. In 1983, there were 83,000 households accepted in England and Wales (Social Trends 1985, Table 8.13). We have already noted that the private rented sector itself is a significant source of such households, which must reflect the fact that they have been unable to find accommodation elsewhere. But perhaps more important is the very large proportion of accepted homeless households – 48% across England overall and 58% in London in 1978 (*Housing and Construction Statistics*, June 1980) – who have not immediately prior to acceptance had a separate home at all, including those living with friends and relations, squatting, living in hostels or hotels or having no accommodation at all. The vast majority of households would qualify for housing benefit to help pay for their housing if they could find private rented accommodation for themselves. Thus there is strong evidence that the private rented sector is not fulfilling its easy access role. Further, the problem is heavily concentrated in London (27% of those accepted in 1978 were housed by London authorities).

14 ii) There are large numbers living in 'non-tenure' accommodation, also concentrated in London.

It is suggested that because of difficulties of access to private renting many households who cannot have recourse to the local authority sector find themselves in 'non-tenure' housing such as hostels, bed-and-breakfast or short-life accommodation.

Evidence of the numbers involved is difficult to evaluate – because it either provides only partial cover of likely cases, or includes other types of households who are adequately provided for but which cannot be excluded. However, some estimates can be made.

First, on Census night in 1981, there were 313,000 persons in England and Wales who were staying in hotels and boarding houses, hostels, common lodging houses and 'miscellaneous communal establishments'. Of these, 153,000 were classified as 'not usually resident' and a further 62,000 were resident staff. Those classified as 'not usually resident' will include some people living permanently in bed-and-breakfast or hostel accommodation as well as genuine non-residents, such as tourists or commercial travellers, but the proportions are unknown. Similarly, resident staff will include a proportion who have taken up the employment wholly or partly in order to obtain somewhere to live (O.P.C.S. 1983e, Table 9). Some idea of the likely proportion can be obtained by looking at the numbers of residents of bed-and-breakfast establishments, hotels, hostels and common lodging houses in receipts of Supplementary Benefit. The DHSS estimate that there were 139,000 such households in 1984 (Conway and

Kemp 1985, p. 17). In addition to these there will be other boarders either in full-time work or not claiming Supplementary Benefit – so total numbers will be higher.

Finally, the Empty Property Unit estimate that there are probably somewhere in the region of 20,000 people living in 'short-life' housing, mainly in London. 'Short-life' housing is poor quality accommodation, usually owned by a local authority or other public body, which would otherwise remain empty, but is let 'on licence' to groups or individuals to use on a temporary basis.

Overall, it seems likely that there are more that 150,000 and possibly as many as 200,000 households in various 'non-tenures' such as bed-and-breakfast, hostel, or short-life accommodation, so the problem of 'non-tenure' accommodation is far from being a marginal or residual issue. For example, the size of this 'sector' may be half the size of the total private renting new lettings market. While one cannot show directly that this phenomenon is related to the difficulty of finding private rented accommodation, it nevertheless remains the case that many of those housed in the 'non-tenures' form part of the traditional demand group for the private rented sector.

The final specific hypothesis is that:

14 iii) There are still many concealed households who are
unable to obtain separate accommodation.

In December 1977, according to the National Dwelling and Housing Survey, there were 253,000 concealed households in England, including 149,000 married couples and 104,000 single parents. Of the married couple concealed households, 72% were either small adult or small family households, and more than 50% of the married couple household heads were aged under 35 (Department of Environment 1979). Survey evidence suggests that more than half of these households will have been living voluntarily with others. However, this estimate does not include any potential single-person households – where, for instance, it is suggested that maybe 70% of sharers desire separate units. Overall, therefore, there was probably at least a quarter of a million potential households that have been unable to find separate accommodation. The 1981 Census is not directly comparable to the NHDS on these variables; however, the evidence suggests, at the very least, that the number of concealed households has not fallen between 1976 and 1981. Since then, relatively low levels of housebuilding, particularly in the public sector, make it unlikely that any progress has been made towards a reduction in this total.

Hence there is very considerable evidence of lack of provision of easy access accommodation which one might expect to be available in the private rented sector. This evidence suggests that the difficulty is mainly concentrated in London, although there are problems in other urban areas and in all areas there are those who cannot alone afford minimal quality housing. Thus while the majority of the decline of the private rented sector probably arises as much from decreased demand as supply, the result leaves many inadequately housed and puts in question the extent to which the private rented sector is fulfilling its easy access role, particularly in economically buoyant areas where the PRS is most needed.

Conclusion with respect to the current situation

Taking the hypotheses about tenants and landlords together thus suggests a picture specified in the following way:

i) The traditional long-term sub-sector remains important but is heavily dependent upon security of tenure legislation for its continued existence. Little or no replacement lettings are being made available for such tenants, at least by profit-oriented landlords.

ii) New supply is mainly only suitable for short-term lets to non-family households.

iii) Those with tenure choice will only choose private renting if its particular attributes are important to them. This group, under present relative subsidy and supply conditions, is concentrated among the young and mobile and its size may continue to decline as other opportunities become more readily available.

iv) Where households have no other choice of tenure, the terms and conditions under which they obtain housing are determined by the state of the market. The size of this group depends more on access and price in the majority tenures than on conditions in the PRS. The extent to which supply is made available depends not just on the costs of provision but also on the effectiveness of controls and the perceived riskiness of the decision to let and returns available elsewhere.

v) The rate of return required by landlords to provide adequate accommodation implies a rent which cannot be paid by most tenants without hardship. This is particularly true in London where there is a concentration both of the types of household which might find private renting acceptable and of those who have no other choice.

1. Note that LFS figures refer to Great Britain, NDHS to England.
2. Excluding employers and housing associations.

Chapter 4 The future of private renting

In examining what the role of the rented sector might be in the future and what might be done to alleviate the difficulties found there, the first requirement is to estimate the number and type of people that might be housed by private landlords over the next decade. A wide range of methods could be used to project changes in the size of the sector. We look first at mechanistic approaches, by which we assume that behaviour in one sense or another remains the same. We then go on to discuss the behavioural factors which might affect these mechanistic predictions and the way that these might change the results.

Demographic-based projections

One of the points which is most often made about the future of the private rented sector is that the demographic changes over the next decade or so will lead to an increase in demand for housing from the types of household that are most likely to require private rented accommodation. Our first exercise therefore is to estimate the size of the sector under the condition that the propensity to rent by household type remains constant but changes are projected in the number of households and the composition of that total in terms of relevant household type.

The Department of Environment publishes household-type projections based on the 1981 Census adjusted for errors found by the post-enumeration survey. These show that there were

18,168,000 households in England and Wales in 1981 (Department of Environment 1985a).[1] Unhappily the household-type categorisation is not consistent between the projection estimates and the published Census material and only the one-person household is fully compatible. However, as this is the most important category from the point of view of the private rented sector and the category where growth is expected to be concentrated, we have simply aggregated the other household types into one.

From the 1981 Census we can calculate the propensity of an household of given type to be in a given tenure. Table 21 shows the propensities for the sub-sectors of the private rented sector for England and Wales. Almost one in five of all one-person households are in the private rented sector but, as we have shown, older households are very much more likely to be in unfurnished accommodation and younger households in furnished.

The next stage is to apply these propensities to the projected estimates of the number of households of each type. The total number of households is expected to increase by nearly 2.5 million in the 20 years after 1981, and over two-thirds of the increase will be among one-person households (Table 22).[2] Because traditional private renting is also concentrated among these households the results show a continuing increase in the two main sub-sectors in both absolute and relative terms. In the job-related sub-sector,

TABLE 21

Propensity to be a private tenant by household type

England and Wales 1981

	Total PRS	Unfurnished	Furnished	Business & Employment
One person households	0.1810	0.1082	0.0632	0.0096
All other households	0.0900	0.0472	0.0187	0.0241
All households	0.1098	0.0605	0.0384	0.0210

Source: 1981 Census

TABLE 22

The numbers in the private rented sector:
1981–based household projection, with constant propensities

England and Wales

				Private rented sector	
Base 1981 (Census)	All tenures	All PRS	Business/ Employment	Unfurnished	Furnished
Single person h/hs	3848	697	37	416	243
All other households	13857	1247	334	654	259
Total	17706	1944 (10.98%)	371 (2.10%)	1070 (6.05%)	502 (2.84%)
Projections (i) *1986*					
Single person h/hs	4744	859	46	513	300
All other h/hs	14227	1280	343	672	266
Total	18970	2139 (11.28%)	389 (2.05%)	1185 (6.25%)	566 (2.98%)
(ii) *1991*					
Single person h/hs	5236	948	50	567	331
All other h/hs	14569	1311	351	688	272
Total	19805	2259 (11.41%)	401 (2.02%)	1255 (6.34%)	603 (3.04%)
(iii) *1996*					
Single person h/hs	5594	1013	54	605	354
All other h/hs	14760	1328	356	697	276
Total	20354	2341 (11.50%)	410 (2.01%)	1302 (6.40%)	630 (3.10%)
(iv) *2001*					
Single person h/hs	5847	1058	56	633	370
All other h/hs	14784	1331	356	698	276
Total	20630	2389 (11.58%)	412 (2.00%)	1331 (6.45%)	646 (3.13%)

Source: 1981 base from 1981 Census
Projections from DOE Household Projections 1981–2001

which is almost wholly made up of multi-person households, there is a slight relative fall although absolutely there is still an increase.

Thus, if current household-type-specific propensities to rent privately were to remain constant, the absolute size of the sector would increase by 23% by 2001 with the furnished sector increasing by 29%.

Because most of the increase in one-person households is expected to be among younger households, it is helpful to develop the forecast further, by dividing the one-person households into those above and below retirement age. We then find a greater increase predicted in the size of the furnished sector. Table 23 shows the propensities to be a private tenant in England in 1981, by age and household type. Table 24 gives the forecast for 1986–2001 for the size of the private rented sector and sub-sectors in England. On this forecast, over the period 1981–2001, the total private rented sector will increase by 24%, and the furnished sub-sector by 31%. It should, however, be remembered that because these propensities are held constant, this mechanistic projection takes no account of cohort effects. These are likely to lead to a decrease in the number of older households in the unfurnished sub-sector.

TABLE 23

Propensity to be a private tenant by age and household type

England 1981

	Total PRS	Business/ Employment	Unfurnished	Furnished
One person working-age households	0.2598	0.0230	0.0851	0.1518
Single pensioner households	0.1412	0.0025	0.1219	0.0168
All other households	0.0910	0.0244	0.0475	0.0191
All households	0.1110	0.0212	0.0609	0.0289

Source: 1981 Census

Because so much of the private rented sector is concentrated in the Greater London area (one-third of the whole sector was within the GLC boundary in 1981) and the majority of pressure is observed in London, it is worth repeating the national exercise for London (Tables 25 and 26). The pattern is basically similar, though less pronounced than for England as a whole, because, although one-person households are proportionately more

93

TABLE 24

The numbers in the private rented sector:
1981-based projections, with constant propensities

England

Base 1981 (Census)	All tenures	All PRS	Business/ Employment	Private rented sector	
				Unfurnished	Furnished
Single person working-age h/hs	1279	332	29	109	194
Single person h/hs	2367	334	6	289	40
All other h/hs	13073	1189	319	621	249
Total	16719	1856	354	1019	483
Projections:					
(i) *1986*					
Single persons < 60	1585	412	36	135	241
Single pensioners	2908	411	7	354	49
All other h/hs	13432	1222	328	638	257
Total	17925	2045 (11.41%)	371 (2.07%)	1127 (6.29%)	547 (3.05%)
(ii) *1991*					
Single persons < 60	1762	458	41	150	267
Single pensioners	3195	451	8	389	54
All other h/hs	13767	1253	336	654	263
Total	18723	2162 (11.55%)	385 (2.06%)	1193 (6.37%)	584 (3.12%)
(iii) *1996*					
Single persons < 60	1907	495	44	162	289
Single pensioners	3385	478	8	413	57
All other h/hs	13952	1270	340	663	266
Total	19245	2243 (11.65%)	392 (2.04%)	1238 (6.43%)	612 (3.18%)
(iv) *2001*					
Single persons < 60	2030	527	47	173	308
Single pensioners	3500	494	9	427	59
All other h/hs	13975	1272	341	664	267
Total	19506 (11.76%)	2293 (2.04%)	397 (6.48%)	1264 (3.25%)	634

Source: *1981 base from 1981 Census*
Projections from DOE Household Projections 1981–2001

TABLE 25

Propensity to be a private tenant by age and household type

Greater London 1981

	Total PRS	Business/ Employment	Unfurnished	Furnished
One person working-age households	0.3499	0.0176	0.1006	0.2317
Single pensioner households	0.2037	0.0018	0.1739	0.0280
All other households	0.1294	0.0165	0.0683	0.0445
All households	0.1656	0.0145	0.0873	0.0638

Source: 1981 Census

important in London than elsewhere, this proportion is expected to rise more slowly in London than elsewhere. Hence, over the period 1981–2001, the number of one-person households in London is expected to rise by 32%, as against 56% in the rest of England, while the total number of households is projected to increase by 12% as against 17%. On the basis of these projections, all sub-sectors increase in both absolute and relative terms (Table 26). The size of the sector overall increases by 18% by 2001, with the furnished sub-sector increasing by 22%.

Thus, perhaps surprisingly, on demographic factors alone, the private rented sector would be expected to grow less in London, both absolutely and as a proportion of the total, than in the country overall. Of course, the validity of this projection depends on the accuracy of the base forecast of London's population and its structure *vis-a-vis* the national forecast. In the past, these have not been particularly accurate. But the *relative* implications arise mainly from the fact that the average size of household is already smaller in London than elsewhere, especially in Central London.

Looking at the results of the mechanistic projections of the effects of demographic change, we find that private renting increases in importance both because of the projected increase in the total number of households and the relative increase in the number of one-person households.

TABLE 26

The numbers in the private rented sector:
1981–based projections, with constant propensities

Greater London

Base 1981 (Census)	All tenures	All PRS	Private rented sector		
			Business/ Employment	Unfurnished	Furnished
Single person working-age h/hs	290	101	5	29	67
Single pens. h/hs	362	74	1	63	10
All other h/hs	1856	240	31	127	83
Total	2508	415 (16.56%)	36 (1.45%)	219 (8.73%)	160 (6.38%)
Projections: (i) *1986* Single persons working-age h/hs	352	123	6	35	82
Single pens. h/hs	437	89	1	76	12
All other h/hs	1956	253	32	134	87
Total	2745	465 (16.94%)	39 (1.42%)	245 (8.93%)	181 (6.59%)
(ii) *1991* Single persons working-age h/hs	379	133	7	38	88
Single pens. h/hs	455	93	1	79	13
All other h/hs	1999	259	33	137	89
Total	2834	485 (17.11%)	41 (1.45%)	254 (8.96%)	190 (6.70%)
(iii) *1996* Single persons working-age h/hs	399	140	7	40	92
Single pens. h/hs	455	93	1	79	13
All other h/hs	1992	258	33	136	89
Total	2846	491 (17.25%)	41 (1.44%)	255 (8.96%)	194 (6.82%)
(iv) *2001* Single persons working-age h/hs	415	145	7	42	96
Single pens. h/hs	444	90	1	77	12
All other h/hs	1960	254	32	134	87
Total	2818	489 (17.35%)	40 (1.42%)	253 (8.98%)	195 (6.92%)

Source: 1981 base from 1981 Census
Projections from DOE Household Projections 1981–2001

96

Projections based on past trends

This does not mean that such an increase will occur. The reasons why it almost certainly will not, are twofold:

(i) the propensity of any given group to become private tenants has considerably decreased over time as demand for other tenures, and the capacity to enter these tenures, has increased. This trend can be expected to continue;
(ii) the private suppliers of rental accommodation may not find it worthwhile to increase provision given current conditions (particularly rates of return), so access can be expected to become more difficult and rents to increase, leading to a further shift in demand away from private renting.

For instance, over the 1971–1981 decade, private renting continued to decline in both relative and absolute terms even though the trends in the total number of households and the relative number of one-person households were similar to those projected for 1981–1996. Over that period that total number of households in England and Wales increased from 16.51 million to 17.71 million, i.e. by 7% . The proportion of these households that included only one person increased from 18% to 22%. Yet private renting decreased from 22% to 11% of all households. Thus the propensity to rent privately fell greatly over this period. For instance, General Household Survey data suggest that between 1971 and 1982 the propensity to rent privately fell by over one-third even for single-person households, and by about a half for family households (Table 29).

Taking these factors into account, it may be valuable to examine what would happen if the changes in the proportion of households that rent privately were to continue to fall in the 1980s and 1990s in the same way that they did over the 1970s. The assumption behind this is that changes in the future will take a similar form to those in the past – in terms of the total number of households, the structure of those households and their propensities to rent privately.

To do this, we first of all estimated a regression line for the relationship between the size of the sector and time based on DoE *Housing and Construction Statistics* data for the whole of Great Britain for the period 1972–1982. This was a linear model, for which the best fit was:

$$Y = 18.95 - 0.61x \qquad (r = -0.997)$$

(size of   (time,
sector)   in years)

This clearly fitted fairly well. However, given the rapidity of decline in the last decade, such a model results in negative values for the private rented sector by 2001. While many commentators would be quite happy with that result, past experience suggests that the rate of decline would itself slow down as the size of the sector gets smaller. We therefore fitted a non-linear function which has the attribute of becoming asymptotic to the x-axis. Visual inspection of the data suggested that the form which best represented the data was $1/y = a + bx$. For all households in the sector this gave:

$$1/y = 0.0491 + 0.0029x \quad (r = 0.9962)$$

This non-linear form also fits fairly well. On this projection, the private rented sector (including Housing Associations) falls to 8% of stock by 1996, and to 7.2% by 2001 (Table 27).

The *Housing and Construction Statistics* series used here do not allow us to separate Housing Association dwellings from the rest of the stock, nor to project separately for unfurnished and furnished sub-sectors, nor for different household types. In order to derive these more specific projections, we have used data from the General Household Survey, making five observations in the years 1971, 1974, 1977, 1979 and 1982. Utilising the same non-linear form, we fitted the following regression lines to the data:

TABLE 27

Stock of PRS/HA dwellings, Great Britain:
Observations 1972–1982,
Projections for 1986, 1991, 1996, 2001

	Observations	
Year		*% of stock*
1972		18.0
1973		17.2
1974		16.5
1975		15.7
1976		15.0
1977		14.5
1978		13.9
1979		13.5
1980		13.0
1981		12.2
1982		11 7

	Projections	
Year	*Linear*	*Non-linear*
1986	9.1	10.5
1991	6.1	9.1
1996	3.0	8.0
2001	Zero	7.2

Source: Housing & Construction Statistics 1972–82

$$1/y = 0.044 + 0.0042x \qquad (r = 0.98)$$
$$\text{for all private tenants}$$

$$1/y = 0.073 + 0.0072x \qquad (r = 0.97)$$
$$\text{for unfurnished tenants}$$

$$1/y = 0.283 + 0.0178x \qquad (r = 0.83)$$
$$\text{for furnished tenants}$$

Using these three equations as the basis for projections, we find that the total size of the sector falls from 10% in 1982 to under 6% in 2001 (Table 28). This forecast rate of decline is reasonably

TABLE 28

Non-linear GHS-based projections

Great Britain

	Total PRS	Unfurnished	Furnished
1986	8.9	5.3	1.8
1991	7.5	4.5	1.5
1996	6.5	3.9	1.3
2001	5.7	3.4	1.2

consistent with actual observations during the early 1980s – if anything it perhaps under-estimates the rate of decline.

Application of a similar approach to regional totals suggests that the largest reductions over the next fifteen years will be found in the North West and the Midlands because of the rapid decline in the mainstream sector.[3] On the other hand, growth in the relative importance of hitherto minor sub-sectors such as employment-related housing (especially of agricultural workers), tourist and retirement accommodation results in a much higher proportion of the sector being located in East Anglia and the South West by the end of the century. Average falls are predicted in the North, Yorkshire and Humberside and the South East.

Another indication of likely changes in the sector can be obtained by examining trends by household type and socio-economic group. For household type, detailed non-linear projections can be made on the same basis as the national ones, again using GHS data. These are presented in Table 29 and give a clear indication of the way in which the propensities of particular household types to live in the private rented sector have changed. Over the eleven years between 1971 and 1982 the propensity to be in the sector decreased greatly for all household types – but for large families it declined twice as much as for single adults of working age. Older single-person households also had a relatively low rate of decline. The propensity of the other household types fell on average by about half.

TABLE 29

Private renting households by household type 1971–82, projections for 1986, 1991, 1996, 2001

Great Britain

% of households who are private renters

	71	74	77	79	82	86	Projections 91	96	2001
1. Singles under 60	40	35	34	31	28	26	23	21	19
2. Small adult h/hs	24	21	15	14	11	9	8	7	6
3. Small family	16	14	11	8	8	6	6	5	4
4. Large family	13	10	7	7	5	4	4	3	3
5. Large adult h/hs	14	11	9	10	8	7	6	5	5
6. Older small h/hs	20	15	12	14	10	9	8	7	6
7. Single 60+	25	20	17	16	15	13	11	10	9
All non-single h/hs (2–6 inclusive)	17	14	11	11	9	8	7	6	5

Note: Projections based on regression analysis using the functional form:

$$1/y = a + bx$$

Slope and intercept values as follows:

	a	b	r
1. Singles under 60	0.02408	0.00093	0.98
2. Small adult h/hs	0.03374	0.00453	0.98
3. Small family	0.5208	0.00650	0.95
4. Large family	0.06137	0.01078	0.98
5. Large adult h/hs	0.07056	0.00441	0.93
6. Older small h/hs	0.4801	0.00398	0.91
7. Single 60+	0.03941	0.00245	0.98
Non-single h/hs (2–6 inclusive)	0.05403	0.00464	0.99

Source: General Household Survey (for 1971–82 data)

101

Projections based on non-linear regression estimates show continuing overall decline, together with a further concentration in the sector of single-person households of working age, and one- and two-person elderly households. (By 1996, single persons of working age will be the only household type with more than 10% in the private rented sector.) Hence, by the end of the century, the much smaller sector would be even more atypical of households in general than it is at present. Other projections suggest that by 1996 over two-thirds of those living in the unfurnished sector would be elderly couples or elderly single persons, while in the furnished sector well over half would be single-person households of working age.

Analysis by socio-economic group can only be done using linear estimates because of a shortage of comparable data. Such projections show a very different pattern for private renting by SEG in the late 1970s compared to the early 1970s. In 1972 the highest levels of private renting were found amongst the semi-skilled and unskilled manual workers (over 20% in both cases). By 1979, the highest levels were among junior non-manual workers. By 1991, a linear projection suggests that the non-manual groups will predominate in the sector, with very low levels of private renting among all types of manual workers. However, a major difficulty with this projection is that it does not allow the separation of those in the labour force from those who are economically inactive – which is currently thought to be the most important variable distinguishing those in private renting from those in the majority tenures (Whitehead and Kleinman 1985). What it does show is the relative growth of non-manual groups, who are often thought to be more mobile. The contribution of the sector to meeting the housing needs of lower-income households on the other hand would appear to be minimal by the end of the century.

Projections based on the assumption that the future can be predicted by extending past trends thus suggest that propensities to rent are likely to continue to decline, but for single people and elderly small households, propensities will decline less rapidly than for other households. Secondly, the propensities of mobile households and those in job-related rented housing are likely to fall relatively slowly. As a result, the composition of the sector will become more homogeneous – with even higher proportions of elderly households in the unfurnished sub-sector and of single adults of working age in the furnished sub-sector. These factors result in greater concentration of the sector in East Anglia, the the South West and to a lesser extent the South East, as the 'traditional' sector continues to decline in other regions. The relative proportions of higher-income and non-manual groups will increase, as the numbers of low-income and manual groups, particularly those in employment, continue to fall.

Synthesis

The final stage of the mechanistic forecast is to integrate the 'demographic' and 'historic' aspects by applying the propensities estimated from the regression equations above, to the DoE projections of different household types. The results are shown in Table 30. These were derived by multiplying the DoE estimates of the numbers of one-person working age households, one-person pensioner households, and other households, by the propensities obtained from Table 29, adjusted by scaling factors to take account of the fact that the General Household Survey refers to Great Britain, while our two forecasts are for England, and for Greater London.

On the basis of this more integrated forecast, we would expect the private rented sector in England to decline by about 10% by 1991, and by about 28% by 2001. By the end of the century, there would be only around 1.3 million households in the sector. The decline in London is expected to be similar to the rest of the country, falling by around 10% by 1991, and by 31% by the end of the century. This would mean around 286,000 households in the private rented sector in London, so that the sector would be

TABLE 30

Projections by age and household type
based on declining propensities

	England		London	
	All tenures	PRS	All tenures	PRS
(i) *1986*				
Single persons under 60	1585	365	352	106
Single pensioners	2908	378	437	83
All other households	13432	1075	1956	235
Total	17925	1818 (10.14%)	2745	424 (15.45%)
(ii) *1991*				
Single persons under 60	1762	352	379	102
Single pensioners	3195	351	455	73
All other households	13767	964	1999	200
Total	18723	1667 (8.90%)	2834	375 (13.23%)
(iii) *1996*				
Single persons under 60	1970	343	399	100
Single pensioners	3385	339	455	64
All other households	13952	837	1992	179
Total	19245	1519 (7.89%)	2846	343 (12.05%)
(iv) *2001*				
Single persons under 60	2030	325	415	91
Single pensioners	3500	315	444	58
All other households	13975	699	1960	137
Total	19506	1339 (6.86%)	2818	286 (10.15%)

THE FUTURE OF PRIVATE RENTING

slightly less concentrated in London in 2001 than it is at present. One-person households would make up 48% of the sector nationally, and 52% of the sector in London in 2001, compared with 36% nationally and 42% in London in 1981. Single-person working age households would increase from 18% to 24% of the sector nationally, and from 24% to 32% of the sector in London.

If we compare this projection with our earlier two projections, which were based separately on demographic changes and on the historical pattern of decline, we find that the integrated projection gives a figure of 6.9% of households in the sector in 2001, as against the estimate of 11.8% based purely on demographic changes, and that of 5.7% (in Great Britain) based solely on extrapolating past decline. We suggest that the figure of 6.9% represents the 'best guesstimate' of the likely size of the private rented sector at the end of the century, and demonstrates how the demographic changes, which suggest an increase in private renting, are far outweighed by the economic and social factors which underlie the continuing decline in private renting this century.

Behavioural factors

This mechanistic approach cannot be expected to provide anything other than a general impression of what might happen if the environment in which housing decisions are made remains constant. In particular, all the variables – changes in the total number of households, in the structure of these households and of the propensity to be in the sector – were affected in the 1970s both by general economic conditions and by the situation in the housing market itself. These conditions will not be replicated in the 1980s and 1990s.

Excluding the demographic aspects we have already taken into account, the types of factors that one might expect to modify demand over the next decades include in particular:

(i) the extent of growth and employment in the economy,

which affects both the capacity to form separate households and the preparedness to pay for housing;

(ii) the relative price and availability of private rented accommodation compared to conditions prevailing in the majority tenures;

(iii) changes in the costs and incentives to move house and their effect on tenure choice and housing decisions;

(iv) social changes in, for example, the extent of marital breakdown;

(v) administrative changes in, for example, the requirements for local authorities to provide accommodation for certain household groups;

(vi) changes in the system of transfer payments with respect especially to housing benefit, supplementary benefit and pensions; and

(vii) changes in the legal framework particularly with respect to the terms and conditions under which rented accommodation is made available.

On the supply side this last factor, (vii), changes in the legal framework, is one of the most important ways in which incentives to let may change. Other variables which would affect the relative rate of return available on letting include changes in:

(viii) the returns available on other types of asset, particularly financial assets; and

(ix) the vacant possession sale price of accommodation arising, for instance, from variations in the demand for owner-occupied housing or from changes in the availability of house purchase finance for different types of property.

These factors, together with the rents that can be charged for rented accommodation, will affect the incentives of private landlords whose motives for letting are directly economic and financial. Those who have other reasons for letting will be affected by different factors including the extent of observed need, the ease of organising the provision of rented accommodation, the landlord's own income, the availability of suitable property and, for employers, the easiest way of obtaining the labour required.

To determine the likely size of the private rented sector over the next decade or so, we need to adjust the mechanistic forecast to take account of these factors with respect to both demand and supply; to estimate the resultant size both of demand and supply under these conditions and finally to assess whether it is demand or supply which is likely to be the constraining factor. In practice, all we can do is suggest which of the variables are likely to operate in which direction and so arrive at some "guesstimate" of the way trends will be modified. Our initial assumption is that if there are no changes the propensity to rent will continue to decline as in the past. We start with demand factors.

(i) Income and employment

Looking first at demand, there are undoubtedly some indications of change. First, while it is predicted that general income levels will continue to rise, perhaps at a faster rate than in the last decade, the extent of long-term unemployment is also still growing and the proportion of households that are economically inactive is expected to increase (Department of Environment 1977b, 1985a). The continuing increase in GNP can be expected further to reduce the demand for private rented accommodation. The concentration of unemployment among the young could have two effects which work in opposite directions. First, it may reduce the capacity of young people to form separate households so that the trend towards leaving home earlier might be reversed. On the other hand, lack of secure earning power might force some non-family households, who would otherwise have been able to find accommodation in the majority tenures, into the private rented sector. Other pressures could include a greater propensity to share accommodation or to find shelter in 'non-tenure' accommodation.

Which of these will actually occur will depend particularly on the form of welfare system available and the cost and availability of accommodation.

Over the last decades, the downward pressure on demand for private renting exerted by increased incomes has been far stronger than any upward pressure arising from the difficulties of particular groups. The future may be different because the composition of the sector is now so concentrated among marginal groups. But perhaps the most important change is likely to be in the extent of household formation itself. Here international evidence (US Bureau of the Census 1983; Australian Bureau of Statistics 1983) has suggested a significant slowdown in the potential to become a separate household. UK evidence is as yet unclear. Overall, the best guess with respect to these particular factors might be that:

(a) demographic forecasts will turn out to have overestimated the growth in households, particularly among those most likely to enter private renting;

(b) the speed of decline in the propensity to rent might well slow down, as is indeed implied by the non-linear mechanistic estimate; and

(c) only if privately rented housing became more readily available would those suffering economic hardship find their way into the sector. Otherwise what growth there is might be concentrated in the 'twilight' areas of non-tenure housing.

So the net effect will be a continuing decline in the demand for traditional private renting, together with a probable increase for multi-occupation and smaller, low quality units.

(ii) *Price and availability*

The second most important factor is the relative cost and availability of other types of accommodation. Over the last two decades local authority housing has become easier to obtain and, over most of the 1970s, rents did not, at least, rise in real terms (Lansley 1979, p. 59; Kleinman et al. 1985, p. 57). Second, owner-occupation became much easier to achieve and those who could afford it found it to be the best possible investment (Kleinman et al., 1985, pp. 36–38; Maclennan, 1982; Merrett, 1982). So all the pressure was away from private renting towards the majority tenures. But here the future may well not be like the past. Most importantly, there has been persistent central government pressure over the last few years to raise the rents of local authority accommodation. If this pressure continues rents, at least in some areas, will reach and perhaps exceed, market levels giving an incentive for those who prefer the attributes of private rental to those of public, or who find that they can obtain a better deal in the private sector, to move to private renting. If rents are continually forced up in the public sector and investment in improvement and repair is limited, for some groups private renting might well become more desirable. The extent of this shift would, of course, depend upon the availability and price of private rented units as well as the extent of the upward pressure on public sector rents.

The other major determining factor is the extent to which the tax and subsidy structure continues to favour owner-occupation. This government sees the extension of owner-occupation as a major plank in their general policy of privatisation (Whitehead, 1983b). While there are many signs that changes in the taxation and financing systems may operate to make housing a less desirable investment, there are as yet few which suggest that, within the housing sphere, there will be any shift away from the emphasis on owner-occupation. Opposition parties might emphasise the provision of social renting rather more but are even less likely than the government to favour private renting.

In this context there seems little reason to expect any shift in demand to private renting arising from changes in the price and availability of owner-occupied housing. If there is increased demand it will come because social renting has become less attractive or less readily available. Under current government policies which have resulted in much lower levels of additions to stock in the public sector and, indeed, a decline in the absolute size of that stock (Cooper 1985, Tables 5.1 and 6.1), this is likely to produce some upward pressure in demand for private accommodation. Such demand is likely to come mainly from non-family households looking for medium- and long-term accommodation, most of whom would probably be better off in the council or housing association sectors, were they able to gain access to them.

(iii) *Mobility*

A major attribute of rented accommodation is its suitability for mobile households. Structural changes in the location and types of employment can be expected to increase the need for such accommodation if adjustment is to be possible – demand can therefore be expected to increase. Similarly, if London and other cities increase their roles as international centres, demand for renting will increase. For instance, over 120,000 households renting privately in 1981 – i.e. 5% of the total – were foreigners of non-Commonwealth origin (O.P.C.S. 1983d, Table 11).

Second, the growth of owner-occupation means that many more households wish to move within that sector. This can be a complex process because of the chains involved – short-term private renting may increasingly be seen as one way of easing the problem.

Third, if real capital gains from owner-occupation became less likely, the incentive for those who expect to be in one location for a relatively short period to own will decline. In the mid-70s the advice to any home-owner was always to buy, even if they were going to move again within a year and even with the high costs of house purchase. In the mid-80s, while some of these costs may themselves have declined in real terms, the relatively modest real gains in house prices may make such purchases undesirable.

110

The types of additional demand for private renting therefore which might be forthcoming as a result of mobility aspects relate mainly to the employed population and often to the relatively well-off. This is consistent with the growth in importance to the sector of non-manual households. What will be required to meet the demand will be reasonable quality accommodation for quite short periods. The demand from poorer migrant households looking for short-term accommodation should, however, also increase because of labour market factors. Such households would presumably be looking for lower cost, lower quality housing from which they would hope to move quite rapidly into the major tenures.

(iv) *Social factors*

There is evidence that the private rented sector continues to cater for a relatively high proportion of households facing sudden changes in their family circumstances, as well as in the longer term for those who are then not able to move back into the major tenures. Increased incidence of, for example, marital breakdown, single parenthood and parents wanting children to leave home could increase the demand for rented accommodation. If this is not met by social agencies such demand will find itself in private renting or non-tenure accommodation. Much of the accommodation required would be of a temporary nature similar to that wanted by other mobile groups. Some people, however, may be looking for long-term accommodation of the traditional type. The extent of such demand would be very much dependent upon the administration and subsidy aspects discussed below.

(v) *Administrative factors*

Local authorities are required to re-house certain priority groups, notably families and pensioners, if they find themselves homeless (Hughes, 1981, pp. 172–173). Changes in these requirements would modify the types of households gaining access

111

to the public sector and therefore the composition of demand for private renting. Whether or not it would change totals, depends on the nature of the change and how the local authorities responded to meet these new requirements. If they were given wider responsibility in regard to all homeless persons, one response could be to substitute one type of household for another, i.e. to re-house a greater proportion through the homelessness channel, and correspondingly fewer through waiting-list or other criteria. In this case the net change in demand for private renting would be small. However, in stress areas, and particularly in London, the scope for such substitution is small, given a declining availability of new and re-lettings, and a relatively high proportion of statutory re-housing commitments. In other areas, although substitution may be possible, local authorities may decide against it for political or other reasons. If instead they meet increased demand by other means, for instance by extending the use of bed and breakfast accommodation, demand for private renting as such would be reduced. However, there are strong social and financial disincentives to such a course of action. Another possibility is that the local authorities' responsibilities toward the homeless would be reduced, and hence their role as a provider of last resort would be diminished, resulting directly in an increase in the demand for private renting, although again the overall effect would depend on whether total local authority supply is reduced as a result. The demand for private renting which might arise from this source would probably be mainly for longer-term secure accommodation similar to that which would have been provided, almost certainly at better quality and with greater efficiency, in the local authority sector.

(vi) *Government assistance*

Housing benefit is available to all households able to find separate accommodation, although the extent of take-up in the private rented sector, especially among mobile households, is still relatively low (McGurk and Raynsford 1984; Kemp and Raynsford 1984). While this system remains, government assistance supports the payment of rents to private landlords and allows those without adequate income to make at least basic demands effective. The system thus props up – however inadequately – the bottom of the housing market.

If assistance via housing benefit were further restricted, as is implied by the 1986 White Paper on the reform of social security – e.g. the proposals to introduce, for those in work, both steeper tapers and a reduction for all claimants in the amount of rates which qualify for rebate, from 100% to 80% (Department of Health and Social Security 1986) – then demand for private renting among lower-income households could be reduced. Already there have been signs of worry from the government about the open-endedness of the commitment, particularly in regard to housing benefit for young people, and there have been some reductions in benefit levels in both 1984 and 1985. If there were a further tightening of eligibility, demand at the lower end of the market could be reduced.[4]

On the other hand, if eligibility requirements remained constant and it became easier to find accommodation, there would undoubtedly be additional households prepared to take up the available units. To this extent supply could create its own demand.

Another relevant aspect of the income maintenance system is the way that pensions and supplementary benefit are made available. At the present time the system allows most owner-occupiers, and local authority tenants, to stay in their own homes as they get older and perhaps poorer. As a result, the price faced by consumers is often lower in the majority tenures so there is hardly any incentive to move down market into private renting to help realise assets or to cut down current housing costs. Large-scale reductions in benefit would be politically highly unpopular – but if they were to take place, demand for private renting might increase as people reduced their demand for housing. There might also be a commensurate increase in supply from older households offering accommodation as resident landlords to help cover their own costs.

(vii)   *The legal framework*

Changes in the terms and conditions of letting would obviously modify the utility obtained from renting privately as compared to other tenures. Most of the effects would come from changes in price and availability, e.g. from the removal of rent control on new lettings which would affect some adversely because prices increased, but might benefit others if access were improved. However, changes such as the introduction of standard contractual arrangements and the removal of forms of non-Rent Act lettings (such as licensing) could make private renting a more attractive proposition for tenants, at least at the margin. However, whether this would translate into effective demand, or would merely regularise the status of certain types of existing letting remains unclear and would depend mainly on its effect on supply (see below pp. 116–117).

Most of the factors which might modify demand that we have discussed are highly speculative. If one compares their possible effect with observed behaviour during the 1970s most suggest that the decline in demand as measured by the changing propensity to rent privately is likely to slow down as a result in particular of:

- lower growth in incomes and higher unemployment among the relevant groups;
- increases in the relative price of social rented housing and reductions in net new supply of such accommodation;
- an increase in the demand for short-term accommodation to provide more flexibility in housing and job decisions;
- the continuation of social trends towards marital and family break-up;
- the continuing provision of income-related benefits both to people without their own resources, enabling them to form

separate households; and to those whose incomes decline, enabling them to continue living separately.

The administrative, legal and financial framework in which decisions are made will also clearly affect demand in ways which will be determined by political pressure and cannot readily be predicted.

The overall picture, taken together with the fact that the size of the private rented sector has now become so small that most of those remaining probably have either quite strong reasons for being there or a lack of realistic opportunities to leave the sector, suggests that propensities to rent are not likely to continue to fall as quickly as they have in the past. On this basis the non-linear assumption applied to the DoE household projections might be a reasonable guess of the lower bound for *demand* for private renting over the next decade (see above, p. 103). It is difficult to imagine any likely circumstance in which the upper bound could be much above that described by the demographic projection based on current propensities. This implies a demand projection for 2001 ranging between 1.3 million and 2.3 million, with a strong bias towards the lower figure.

The discussion about the likely sources of increased demand has implications for the types of dwellings that might be demanded. Some households would be looking for good quality short-term accommodation, while many would be prepared, or forced, to accept poorer quality, smaller, perhaps shared units. Furthermore, if the provision of social rented units declines and prices increase, there could also be an upturn in the demand for long-term secure accommodation. These factors, taken together with the demographic pressures, imply a continuing shift away from the demand for traditional unfurnished accommodation towards furnished units both of good quality for the mobile employed and of a lower, cheaper standard mainly for single persons and non-family groups outside the labour force. Only if there is significant structural change in relative subsidy and availability of accommodation between tenures could one expect a revival of the demand for the traditional private rented sector. On the other hand, such projections could always be confounded by other factors. In particular, increasing rates of growth of income in the economy would almost certainly further reduce demand significantly.

Supply factors

The fact that certain demands may increase (or not decline as rapidly as in the past) does not mean that the supply will be forthcoming to meet these demands. Over the last few years there has been every evidence of a continuing decline in the numbers of units landlords wish to make available. The most rapid decline has been concentrated in the traditional protected sector, but in addition there is no evidence of significant activity in the less controlled areas with the number of new lets apparently falling from about half a million in 1976 to 300,000 in 1981 (see above, page 74). Again, there are a number of factors which could change, modifying the likely supply over the next decade.

(viii)   *The effect of legislative change on supply*

There is much discussion at the present time about the possibility of removing rent control and security of tenure from new lettings in order to increase the supply of private rented accommodation (National Federation of Housing Associations, 1985). Whether or not such a change would result in a significant increase in supply depends on a number of important factors (Whitehead 1983a). First, as we have discussed, it can be argued that the majority of new lettings are already either formally or informally outside the Rent Acts. Increased supply would therefore only occur if the terms and conditions faced by landlords improved as a result of legislative change. The most obvious change would be that, while the new legislation remained in force, there would be no fear that the landlord would find that a protected tenancy had been inadvertently created, or that the tenant had obtained a registered "fair" rent. Given that the majority of new lets are now a matter of agreement and might well *in principle* be covered by the Rent Acts (even though the majority of the landlords and tenants concerned do not consider them to be so), the removal of this uncertainty could provide an important additional incentive to supply. Against this would be the fear that any change of government would result in the re-introduction of controls. Unless all-party agreement on the form of new legislation can be obtained, this would undoubtedly militate against the increased incentive to supply.

Second, the removal of rent controls would allow rents to be increased in some parts of the market, thus improving the rate of return available on private renting. As the British Property Federation stated in evidence to the Select Committee, "however much rent levels were increased – by however small an amount or however large an amount – every sort of step would bring some landlords in" (House of Commons Environment Committee 1982b, p. 292). Yet the evidence that we have given in Chapter 3 suggests that rents would have to rise very considerably before this would even halt decline. Even in the Central London "luxury" market, where rents are entirely market determined, the rental return is estimated to be only between 5 and 8% – not enough to induce additional investment for rental income alone (Mitchell 1985). Outside this market, consumers are very unlikely to be able to pay the rents commensurate with this sort of return even with the assistance of housing benefit. Those who could afford it are more likely to continue to choose to own rather than rent.

Thus increased rents and lesser security might well induce some increase in new lets – but the evidence suggests that even to keep up supply to existing levels would require rents well above current market determined levels. Any absolute expansion would have to be generated by fairly high increases in demand, which do not seem likely.

(ix) *Returns on renting in relation to other assets*

Property has always been regarded as a low-risk long-term investment. In the past, controls on rent and security have lowered the return available in comparison to other assets so that traditional investors in such assets have not been prepared to be involved. Pension funds, insurance companies and large property companies have therefore shown very little interest in this area. If expectations were to change there could be an incentive for quite large investments in property in order to obtain the type of diversified portfolios that such institutions would normally desire. However, without government intervention such a response would be dependent upon there being demand from mainstream types of households who could be expected to provide a secure stream of rental payments. Within the current framework this seems unlikely, except perhaps for some additional demand from mobile employed households.

The investment choices available to potential individual landlords have generally widened over the last few years. There is no reason to expect there to be any reversal in this trend, although the real rates of return on financial assets may currently be higher than the long-run equilibrium level. It therefore appears that there are few external reasons why one might expect investment in rental property to become more desirable. That must come from increases in the rents and capital gains available from private renting which again depend upon increases in demand.

One possibility currently under discussion is either transferring property from the local authority sector at prices which would enable an acceptable return to be made or the government guaranteeing the stream of income to financial institutions so that they are prepared to invest in the sector (National Federation of Housing Associations 1985b). The majority of this discussion is within the context of Housing Associations, so it would not increase the supply of privately rented accommodation as here defined. Nor where it involved transfers from the local authority stock would it increase the total supply of rented housing. Only if

118

large scale additional finance were made available by private institutions would it significantly affect the market and this seems unlikely at the present time (but see Chapter 6 below).

(x) *House prices*

There are two different aspects involved here. First, if landlords are able to realise their assets at vacant possession prices (e.g. if security is limited or rents are at market levels), there may be an incentive to invest in domestic property like any other investment and buy and sell such property whenever it seems desirable. (The maximum amount of investment that can be induced in this way would occur with freely determined rents and contractual arrangements.) But the second factor is the rate of return available on housing in its other main use: owner-occupation. While taxation arrangements differ between landlords and owner-occupiers and between tenants and owner-occupiers, the price than can be achieved for most property will be greater in the owner-occupied sector than in private renting (Maclennan 1982; Nevitt 1966). Any given relative subsidy position will result in an equilibrium relationship between the two sectors. At the present time the evidence is that such an equilibrium has not yet been reached, i.e. with full adjustment the size of the private rented sector would be smaller. Landlords still have an incentive to transfer property to owner-occupation unless demand for their particular type of property is depressed in the owner-occupied sector or rents in the private rented sector can be achieved which are high enough to offset the difference in capital values. For the vast majority of traditional property this is still not the case. Where the equilibrium split may have already been achieved is with respect to older, poor quality, property in non-stress areas, and to multi-occupation units in areas of high demand for rented accommodation. The first might meet some types of long-term demand as well as providing for large adult households. The availability of the second will only increase if rents rise. This could

119

anyway choke off some of the potential demand.

Overall, where landlords are looking for financial returns there seems little reason to expect any structural change in the incentive to supply private rented accommodation. Only if rents rose or terms and conditions became more favourable to landlords in other ways would there be any slowdown in the rate of decline in supply. As with demand, and in part because of the demand projections, there may well be factors which suggest that the decline will be less rapid in the future than in the past. There might indeed be some areas of expansion, mainly in areas of overall low demand or as a result of increased pressure on the sector, and therefore higher rents and possibly lower quality of provision.

A significant minority of landlords do not let wholly, or even sometimes at all, for economic reasons (Paley 1978). Predicting changes in their behaviour is probably even more difficult than predicting economic variables. The sort of factors which might be relevant are the growth of second-home ownership which could be let out for part of the year; inheritance of owner-occupied property which the legatees then rent out; the increased desire for communal living, and many other possibilities.

Finally, the provision of job-related accommodation will depend both on what happens to employment in the relevant industries (in the main it is expected to continue to decline) and the ease with which other types of accommodation can be made available. As owner-occupation spreads further down the income scale and the proportion of employed persons who are owner-occupiers rises, the perceived need for job-related accommodation except for the mobile is likely to continue to decline.

Thus on the supply side the picture appears fairly bleak, with continuing decline in the provision of all types of property unless rents are increased significantly; in many areas this would mean rents above those currently prevailing in the uncontrolled sector. This implies that it will be supply which is the constraining factor and demand will only be met if people are prepared to pay far more than at present. This picture would not be significantly changed even by large scale transfers from the public sector stock because, although this would technically increase the size of the sector, practically it has no effect on total supply.

Turning back to the list of possible reasons why demand might be expected to increase, there appears to be some very limited scope for increased rents, if income-related benefits remain at current rates, mainly because of reduced public sector availability. In addition, there seems no reason why accommodation for mobile employed people should not be fairly readily available so some additional units might be provided for this purpose. This does not imply any revival in the fortunes of the private rented sector, just a slowdown in the rate of decline and a continuing shift from traditional provision to short-term, usually multi-occupied, accommodation, together with a better quality sector for the mobile employed.

The most important conclusion for policy purposes is that without very significant changes in condition there will continue to be a shortage of adequate accommodation for poorer households. Indeed the squeeze on this part of the private rented sector could well increase, resulting in more households forced to live in 'non-tenure' accommodation such as bed and breakfast accommodation, hostels, 'squats' and the like. The gap between the reasonably well housed (even within the private rented sector) and those who cannot find adequate accommodation of any type is thus likely to increase.

PRIVATE RENTED HOUSING IN THE 1980s AND 1990s

1. One-person households were apparently under-enumerated in the Census by 7% – mainly because of misclassification between sharing one-person households and large adult households. A high proportion of these households are located in the private rented sector.
2. Note that our 1981 base is taken from the 1981 Census figures, and not from the Department of Environment adjusted figures.

3. Because detailed regional evidence is only available for two dates, 1972 and 1982, it is only possible to use a linear projection. However, this is adequate to show up relative changes between regions if not to provide absolute values.

4. There is an additional complication here arising from the growth of board and lodging accommodation. As eligibility for help towards this type of accommodation is restricted, it becomes harder to form a separate houshold, but where household formation *is* possible, it may be more likely that such households will find themselves in the private rented sector rather than in the "twilight' tenures. However, the difference between the two may mean no more than, e.g. the installation of a cooker in a bedroom, to turn a "boarder" into a "tenant". Thus changes in the regulations may transfer both units and households between sub-sectors.

Chapter 5 Who might the sector serve?

So far we have described the conditions currently obtaining in the private rented sector, analysed the role of the sector in the overall housing market, examined various hypotheses about how it operates and made an attempt at forecasting its likely size and composition over the next ten to fifteen years. In this section, we look at a slightly different question: what role might private renting suitably play in a system which aims to provide accommodation for all? To do this we go back to the attributes of tenure and look first at the advantages and disadvantages of renting versus owning, and then at any advantages and disadvantages specific to the choice between *private* and *public* renting. We would stress here that in this section we are going back to 'first principles', and working through the *theoretical* arguments about tenure choice. To this extent, therefore, the discussion takes place at one remove from the realities of the British private rented sector that we have detailed in our first three chapters. This is a necessary stage because questions about tenure choice are rarely spelled out but are basic to the debate about private renting.

Next we look at the constraints on that choice which arises from the way the existing housing system, particularly the subsidy framework, operates. In this way we are able to examine the types of factors which are distorting choices and making it difficult to achieve desirable housing objectives. Finally we ask similar questions with respect to supply – who *a priori* would wish to provide private rented accommodation and on what conditions?

Renting versus owning

Different tenures have different attributes which relate in particular to who owns, manages and finances the assets and to what end. Those who favour particular attributes are therefore likely to be predisposed to choosing the form of tenure which provides them, although because housing as a good is made up of a wide range of attributes, the final choice will require the consumer to make trade-offs between them.

The types of attribute which in principle make renting more desirable to certain household groups relate to the fact that the asset is owned and managed by someone else, so that the commitment to housing can be less in a number of specific ways than for owner-occupiers. These commitments can be broken down into three main groups: transaction costs, maintenance and ownership of the asset. With respect to the first, renting generally has lower financial costs of access than owner-occupation. Transaction costs in the owner-occupied sector are high, as fees or commissions have to be paid to a range of 'exchange professionals' such as solicitors, estate agents and financial intermediaries, as well as to meet statutory requirements with respect to the transfer of property such as stamp duty (Gray 1982a). Access costs for renting only have to cover consumption aspects – finding the accommodation and entering into the rental contract. In some cases the landlord may provide not only accommodation but also furniture and fittings, obviating the tenant's need to meet the financial commitment of ownership of such items.

A second aspect is that renting can have advantages of speedier access. The requirements that the tenant is looking for cover a narrower range than for owner-occupation so search should in principle be easier. Also, if the dwelling is empty, the new tenant can move in almost immediately. In contrast, the finding of a suitable new home in the owner-occupied sector is only the beginning of a process of arranging a mortgage, having the property surveyed, carrying out a search etc, all of which can delay the process by up to several months, or even more where 'chains' of sales must be completed together (Merrett, 1982). The low transaction costs associated with renting also allow the individual household greater freedom to adjust to changes resulting from the family life-cycle, to sudden changes in family or employment circumstances or simply to changing preferences. In this context many owner-occupiers, particularly those moving long distances, frequently undergo a temporary period of renting (usually in the private sector) while arranging the sale of one property and the purchase of another. Generally, households in the rental sector can more speedily adjust the amount that they pay for housing in response to changes in their financial circumstances.

With respect to the second group, tenants do not have the responsibility for repairs and maintenance of their accommodation. This advantage can be expected to be particularly important for two sorts of households – those, mostly younger, households wanting temporary and flexible housing arrangements, the focus of whose lives is usually outside the home; and older households who have neither the physical ability nor the financial resources to maintain the fabric of the house. The advantage of renting is again twofold – first, that the household does not have the responsibility, or worry, of maintaining the home, supervising repair works etc, and second that they do not have to bear the direct financial costs of carrying out repairs (although the upkeep of the dwelling will often be reflected in the rent).

With respect to the separation of ownership from consumption of the asset there are also a number of benefits. First, it is often easier to deal with the indivisibility of housing via rental rather than ownership arrangements. Because the value of the asset relates to the whole unit it is difficult to break up ownership. In contrast, renting can be more flexible in terms of the type of property available and the actual living arrangements. Single people, for example, may require only a single room, preferring to pay a low rent for a small amount of space and spend their money on other commodities or activities. Alternatively, several single people may wish to live semi-communally. This can reasonably

125

readily be organised among renters but the contractual difficulties
if each owed part of the dwelling are likely to be very great because
the behaviour of each would affect the value of the asset to the
others.

Most important of all, by renting rather than owning, the tenant
avoids tying up resources in the housing asset which he or she
might rather spend elsewhere. For low income households in
particular there may be very little incentive to invest in an asset
and tie up current income either for one's own future use or for
those who will inherit, as is required if one is an owner-occupier.
For those with resources, renting gives greater flexibility in
investment decisions and allows tenants to invest in other assets
which may have higher returns or more suitable attributes for the
particular individual.

Overall, renting allows the tenant to take account of a much
shorter time horizon when making decisions, and enables the
tenant to tie up less resources, both financial and managerial, and
to take on fewer responsibilities as well as providing greater
flexibility in response to change.

On the other hand, the separation of ownership and occupation
is seen by many as an inherent disadvantage of renting because
they argue that many of the attributes of housing which are
generally required stem only from ownership. For a tenant, the
property cannot be used or enjoyed for as long as the occupier
wants, nor is there a right to sell it, to give it away, or to enable
heirs to inherit. Although security of tenure, in both the private
and public sectors, and the existence, in certain instances, of rights
of succession go some way towards giving tenants some of the
characteristics of ownership, the tenant remains inferior to the
owner in this respect.

What the tenant has instead is a contractual relationship with
the owner, defined within a given legislative framework, by which
the rights and duties of both parties are specified. Within this
framework it is of course possible to transfer rights from one party
to another, either freely or for a financial consideration – such

transfers are attributes of many forms of intermediate tenure. Alternatively, government may legally transfer rights to the tenant by, for example, imposing security or succession legislation. However, even when such rights are transferred, these tend to be seen as permitted rights, bestowed by central government or the local authorities, and hence liable at some future point to be rescinded or at least curtailed by the same authorities. The ideology of a 'property owning democracy' helps to sustain the notion that rights issuing from property ownership have a fundamental character which provides a refuge from encroachment by state bureaucracy at either the national or the local level, to which, some argue, all aspire.

Another particularly relevant aspect is that the right significantly to modify the dwelling usually lies with the owner rather than the occupier because it affects the value of the asset. As a result, in most cases the tenant's ability to alter his or her immediate environment is limited to decoration, choice of furniture, and perhaps some fixtures and fittings such as shelves. The owner-occupier, in contrast, within the constraints of his or her own skills and financial resources, is restricted only by the demands of planning and building legislation. Council tenants who buy their own homes frequently give as one of their reasons for buying their frustration with council prohibitions of structural changes, or even minor forms of redecoration – the archetypal uniformity of colour of front doors. It has become a cliche that council houses that have been bought by their occupiers are readily identifiable on council estates by a variety of minor and major changes that have been made to the structure, ranging from new doors and windows to back extensions and patios. The disadvantage that tenants – both private and public – feel in this regard in relation to owner-occupiers is two-fold. Not only are many tenants prevented from altering their homes in any fundamental way, but even in those cases where landlords allow such activities the tenant feels less inclined than the owner to carry out the changes because any financial benefit resulting from

127

improvement will accrue to the owner of the asset, the landlord, and not to the occupier. Many of the benefits of owner-occupation flow not just from ownership *per se* but from the 'jointness' of ownership and occupation. In particular, owner-occupation removes the contractual relationship which, because of the potentially divergent interests of owners and occupiers, is likely to be a major source of conflict. The two main reasons for these difficulties are:

(i) the way the dwelling is used by the tenant can adversely affect its asset value and so reduce the owner's wealth. Specifying the contract to take account of the possibilities, monitoring the problems, evaluating their effect on the asset value and enforcing contractual responsibilities can be both difficult and costly. Conversely, if a tenant actively improved the value of the asset he or she may find it difficult to obtain suitable compensation;

(ii) in many instances the benefit to the occupier increases with time spent in the dwelling because, for instance, the locality becomes familiar, social relationships are built up, or small changes specific to the tenant are made in the property. This creates additional value specific to that tenancy which the owner may attempt to realise by raising the rent, i.e. because of the specificity of the asset there may exist economic rent which is likely to be the subject of not necessarily amicable negotiation (Evans 1985, p. 146.)

These contractual problems arise because of the complex nature of housing and the range of benefits it provides. The extent of their importance will of course vary between different types of contract and owner – but these problems can only be removed altogether by removing the need for a contract as is the nature of owner-occupation.

So far we have looked at the benefits of owner-occupation in comparison to renting in fairly formal terms, concentrating on their inherent attributes. In addition, there are many other differences, most of which favour owner-occupation, which are not inherent but arise from the nature of our housing system.

First, contractual conditions with respect to timing and method of payment are often more rigid for tenants than for owner-occupiers. The owner-occupier can choose from a range of mortgage schemes (standard repayment, endowment, low-start, index-linked etc) and can decide how much to borrow and over what period to pay it back (Boddy, 1980; Merrett, 1982). Moving owner-occupiers, for example, can vary the proportions of the purchase price funded from internal savings and from capital borrowed on mortgage. Of course for many buyers – particularly first-time buyers and marginal purchasers – such choice is more apparent than real, as home ownership may only be possible with very high percentage mortgages, and with little choice with regard to the source or form of mortgage finance. However, the freedom does exist for many owners; moreover, many first-time buyers will expect to have more choice later on, as their equity in the house increases. This contrasts strongly with the position of the tenant who is obliged contractually to pay rent every week or month, has no choice about the method of payment and who in most instances does not participate in any real bargaining process with the landlord. The position of households facing mortgage and rent arrears can also be contrasted. Households facing mortgage arrears usually have a range of options open to them including: getting the lender to accept interest only payments, capitalizing the arrears, or extending the term. Especially when the owner-occupier has a reasonable stake in the equity there is little risk to the lender and terms are often quite generous. Tenants on the other hand often face very rigid arrears and eviction policies and are dependent upon the landlord's goodwill to enable them to keep their home in times of sudden financial crisis.

Second, the tenant has less choice in terms of the types of dwellings available. The owner can choose between a range of different dwellings within a budget constraint. So, for example, a prospective buyer can decide between a two-bedroom house near the city centre, against say a three-bedroom house in a more peripheral location for the same price. He or she can choose, depending on their taste, between a modern newly-built home and an older property, in poorer repair, but with more 'character'. In the rented sector, choice is very much more restricted. The range of property available in the local authority sector is anyway narrower – particularly with respect to location and type, including large numbers of unpopular designs such as tower blocks and deck-access flats. But more importantly, local authorities usually give prospective tenants only two, or at most three, choices, and these are based primarily on the authority's assessment of the applicant's needs, rather than on the applicant's own preferences. Hence tenants do not usually have the opportunity of choosing, for example, to pay more rent for more space; or to have less space in exchange for a central location.

The types of properties found in the private rented sector are generally even more restricted and less desirable. The sector contains a concentration of sub-standard dwellings in terms of disrepair, lack of amenities and sharing of both amenities and rooms. The majority are located in central areas and built before 1919. Most importantly, supply in stress areas is often so limited that prospective tenants have little real choice at all. There is one offsetting factor here: the greater availability of rented dwellings located near the centre of cities and conurbations in comparison to owner-occupied property. Such locations may be attractive to certain household types, particularly young people, for whom access to employment and entertainment is more valuable than other amenities and space. Under a free market regime, the cost of providing housing in such locations is likely to force lower-income households – many of whom depend on access to the central city service sector for employment – either out of the market or into sub-divided and overcrowded apartments. One of the roles of the public rented sector is to make it possible for such groups to live in areas of high demand. Also much of the private rented sector is located near the centre of urban areas, particularly in London. It usually provides lower quality accommodation than is available in the owner-occupied sector but does allow the consumer a trade-off between access and other attributes. Hence renting – both public and private – has an advantage over buying for certain types of household with particular locational requirements.

Overall, while it can be argued that in principle tenants could be given the same choices as owner-occupiers, the way in which the rented sectors have developed means that in many cases they will remain at a disadvantage unless there is considerable new-build for rent, or switching of existing stock between tenures. Only with respect to central location and small non-self-contained units does renting have a significant advantage in comparison to owner-occupation.

Third, and ironically, mobility appears to be more difficult for many tenants than for owner-occupiers. While greater mobility should and could be an *advantage* of renting (see above, pp. 124–5), at present the reverse often seems to be the case. In particular, the restricted availability of rented dwellings makes it difficult for tenants to move between areas. In the public sector, tenants who move into a new area will often go to the bottom of the waiting list of that authority, unless they can obtain a 'mutual exchange' or qualify under the National Mobility Scheme. Private tenants moving to a different area have to compete with other hopefuls in the private rental market, and are initially disadvantaged, as newcomers, by their lack of access to the local information networks – the 'grapevine' – through which a considerable number of new private lettings are made. Moreover, the financial costs of access are often quite large in relative terms, including agency fees, a 'landlord's deposit' plus perhaps a month's rent in advance. While these costs are small in comparison to transaction costs in the owner-occupied sector, they can represent a considerable outlay for many of the households who form the demand group for private renting (House of Commons Environment Committee 1982c, pp. 4–5).

While mobility within a local area is high among tenants, much of it arises from decisions made by the landlord rather than the tenant. Evidence from the early 1970s showed that at least 11% of all local transfers in the public sector were 'forced', while among those moving from private to council renting the proportion was three times higher at 34% (Department of Environment 1977b, Tables II.42 and II.44).

Fourth, the tenant is at a disadvantage compared to the owner as far as access to credit is concerned. This disadvantage is of two kinds. In the first place, the owner-occupier, if he is a mortgagor, has access to a very favourable form of credit, which combines the virtues of being fairly readily available, repayable over an extremely long term, and partly tax-deductible. Furthermore, a considerable portion of this mortgage money 'leaks out' of the housing finance system and is used for other forms of consumption (Bank of England 1982). Additionally, the owner-occupier – whether mortgagor or outright owner – will generally have easier access to other forms of credit, such as loans from banks or finance companies because housing is regarded as a very secure asset against which to lend. Indeed, lenders often actively seek out owner-occupiers and encourage them to borrow. Thus tenants with apparently similar attributes have to pay a higher rate of interest on borrowed money than an equivalent owner-occupier because the signal of ownership gains unequal access to the finance market (Spence 1975). Throughout the 1970s this unequal access was extremely valuable because the capital market was heavily out of equilibrium and real interest rates were negative. In part as a result of these capital market imperfections, it is undoubtedly the case that owner-occupation has in the past provided perhaps the best return on investment available to individuals (Kleinman et al. 1985, pp. 36–38; Maclennan 1982; Merrett 1982). Tenants have therefore clearly been disadvantaged by not being able to accumulate wealth at the same time as consuming housing in the way that owner-occupiers have been able to do, and by having a lower capacity to borrow and a narrower range of lower return investments in which they could invest.

These benefits have been reinforced for existing owner-occupiers by the relative assistance given to them by government taxation and subsidy policy. Owner-occupiers receive mortgage interest relief but do not pay either capital gains tax or tax on the imputed income from their property. Tenants on the other hand have to pay tax on their income and capital gains and will generally not be able to obtain tax relief on any borrowing (Whitehead 1980; Hughes 1979; Atkinson and King 1980; Ermisch 1984). There is thus a strong incentive within the general tax system to become an owner-occupier. In the 1970s the interaction between the tax system and the increasing rate of inflation increased that incentive significantly. Thus, even where a household may have had many of the attributes which would otherwise make it more desirable to rent, the potential for investment in owner-occupation together with the access to specific capital has meant that owner-occupation has been the sensible choice.

However, this does not indicate that renting must always, and necessarily, be inferior to owning in this regard. One can – at least in principle – envisage a combination of tax and subsidy arrangements which would provide for fair treatment between tenures, together with an adequate capital market giving equal access to owners and tenants with similar risk profiles. In this case, choice between tenures would be based on the relative efficiency of production between tenures and the different preferences of households with different attributes. However, such a regime seems a long way off at present; moreover, even were housing finance reform to proceed to such a point, it would probably take several years of such a system operating, and being seen to operate, fairly between tenures before renting ceased to be perceived as financially disadvantageous vis-a-vis owning.

This perception relates to a final practical disadvantage that many tenants experience – the stigma of renting. Most post-war housing policy, as implemented by both major parties, has been predicated on the assumption that home-ownership is a 'natural' or 'basic' human desire (Gray, 1982b, pp. 268–269; Malpass and

Murie, 1982, p. 11). Since 1979 the emphasis on a 'property-owning democracy' has been increased by the Conservative government. As a consequence, tenancy is increasingly seen as a sign of failure, perhaps even as a sign that one has failed to take responsibility for one's own life. This stigma is reinforced by housing policies that support owner-occupation, in particular the additional subsidies available via the Right to Buy and other 'low-cost home ownership initiatives', as well as increases in council rents and the reduction in public sector new-build. The result is that most households who can, try to become owner-occupiers. Renting – both public and private – becomes dominated by those unable to gain access to owner-occupation, especially those outside the labour process: the unemployed, the sick and disabled, pensioners, students and single parents (Forrest and Murie 1984a; English 1982; Robinson and O'Sullivan 1983).

Thus many of the benefits that should be associated with renting – freedom of choice and to change that choice, freedom to invest elsewhere or not to invest at all, and freedom to choose not to involve oneself directly in the management and maintenance of the housing asset – are not in practice available in the rented sectors, either public or private.

Given these constraints and the advantages of owner-occupation that we have specified, it seems likely that a majority of households will continue to prefer this form of tenure. These advantages relate to the inherent difficulties of the letting contract, and the consequent potentiality for conflict between landlord and tenant. Owner-occupation transcends rather than resolves this conflict,[1] and owner-occupiers receive a set of benefits flowing from the peculiar 'jointness' of owner-occupation, i.e. from the fact that owner-occupied housing has the attributes both of an investment and a consumption good, although it must be remembered that there are many low income owner-occupiers who receive few of the benefits which are in general associated with owner-occupation (Karn et al. 1985). Even so, there are households who are likely to find renting more suitable than owning because of their household structure, the stage in their life-cycle and the location and type of accommodation available. In addition, there are many who, given their resources and other circumstances, cannot expect to become owner-occupiers. The next question to be asked with respect to these groups is: are there reasons why renting from a private landlord will be better than renting from the public sector?

Private versus public renting

There are certain advantages that might in principle be expected to flow from renting from a private rather than a public landlord. First, the private sector may be less bureaucratic, anonymous and impersonal than the public sector, which is identified both with vast monotonous housing estates, and with a labyrinthine bureaucratic structure, making it difficult for the tenant to find out exactly which official is responsible for the management of his or her dwelling. Relationships in the private sector might be more personal, with the possibility that the landlord would know his tenants' circumstances and equally the tenants knowing to whom to go when there are problems. (There are of course some very large private sector landlords, but these are now comparatively few. In any event, they have never approached the size of the largest public sector landlords.) This closer proximity between landlord and tenant may result in a better relationship between them (although, equally, the reverse may be true, as we discuss below, page 139). This can be contrasted with the situation in the public rented sector where not only is responsibility shared between a variety of officials, perhaps in different local authority departments, but also, even when decisions are taken they have to be communicated through several intermediaries before being put into effect.

It might also be argued that the private landlord has a more direct incentive to maintain his property in good condition and to be responsive to tenants' preferences than a public landlord because of his concern to protect the return on his investment. Enlightened self-interest on the part of the landlord may be a better guarantee of the welfare of the tenants than supposedly democratic control exercised by the community, which in practice often tends to be bureaucratic and unresponsive. Essentially, this is a specific case of the general argument in favour of the market rather than planning. The argument against it is that for the landlord it may often be financially more desirable to let the property deteriorate when there are better investments elsewhere. This has been the more usual experience over the century at least at the lower end of the market, and is indeed a major reason for the establishment of a large public sector (Malpass and Murie 1982, Chapter 2; Gauldie 1974; Burnett 1978). More generally, the need to respond flexibly to consumer demand depends upon equilibrium or excess supply in the market. Over the century the major experience has been of excess demand at the lower end of the market and often very limited attempts to meet requirements.

Third, private renting, at least from non-resident landlords, may offer more privacy than the public sector. Private landlords are likely to be far less concerned about, for example, under- and over-occupancy, sub-letting, keeping pets etc. than public landlords as long as the rent is paid regularly and objections from neighbours do not reach the landlord. Thus private sector management may be less intrusive. This may also be true of access and letting procedures. To qualify for a council house, one has usually to fill in lengthy forms, answer questions of a personal nature and perhaps be visited in one's present accommodation by a council official (who may assess 'housekeeping standards') as part of the allocation procedure. Then one has to wait while a decision is made by officials unknown to oneself (Gray 1979). In contrast, the procedure in the private rented sector will usually be quicker and less bureaucratic. Interviews are usually on an informal basis, and the landlord rarely requires much more information than that necessary to satisfy himself that the applicant will be able to pay the rent and look after the property.

Fourth, the flexibility of the private sector may offer scope for 'non-commercial' type arrangements. These will include lettings to family and friends, where the economic return is not the primary consideration. In some cases, there may be some level of social or emotional support, such as for a sick or elderly relative, who can have some independence by renting a room or even a self-contained flat within a larger dwelling. A significant proportion of lettings within the private rented sector are made for reasons unrelated to profit (e.g. 12% of lettings in the 1978 Survey [Todd et al. 1982] were rent-free) and many others are beneficially affected by the personal relationship between landlord and tenant.

A different type of flexibility arises from the way a given dwelling can be assigned among different households. Resident landlords provide quite a different type of accommodation from that available in the majority sectors, as do dwellings broken up into non-self-contained units. This type of accommodation may be particularly suitable for certain types of households who want some communal living arrangements as well as for single persons and others who want limited housing sevices. Again, problems arise when this type of accommodation is all that is available for households looking for separate and secure accommodation. But this does not detract from the fact that some households are best served in this way and that such arrangements are difficult within the more formal requirements necessitated by mortgagees or public sector accountability.

Finally, if renting is stigmatised, the private rented sector may carry less "stigma" than the public sector because it is less obvious. Private tenancies are usually scattered through the housing stock, streets often containing a mixture of owner-occupied and rented property. Private rented property is rarely concentrated on estates. Even where it is, these are often of a high-status 'up-market' nature and/or are partially owner-occupied. Some potential tenants may therefore prefer private renting because the accommodation is likely to be a 'proper house' (or at least part of a 'proper house') in an ordinary residential street, rather than a public sector tenancy on an estate, particularly where the estate is of a non-traditional built form such as deck-access, etc.

Thus the potential benefits of private as opposed to public renting can be expected to flow from greater flexibility – in access, in the type of accommodation, in the way the property can be used, and in the relationship between landlord and tenant. Tenants could in principle expect greater choice of accommodation and a more responsive and efficient landlord than in the public sector. However, these benefits will only be realised where tenants have reasonable power to make their desires felt in the market. This raises two types of problem: (i) those which are inherent in the landlord-tenant relationship; and (ii) those which arise from the landlord's relative power either because of lack of capacity to pay on the part of the tenant, or because of shortages of accommodation.

The inequalities in the relationship between landlord and tenant result from their different objectives, together with the difficulties of monitoring and enforcing the contract. These are inherent in the commercial private rented sector where landlords can be expected to wish to maximise profit. Quite apart from the specific conflicts and inequalities arising from external constraints such as rent control and security of tenure, more general conflicts arise because the tenant's interests as a consumer are often directly contradictory with those of the landlord as investor. Arguments about equity in the PRS – whether security is 'unfair' to the landlord, how much is a 'fair' rent, etc – have continued for decades. They are in the final analysis insoluble because what can be agreed to be 'fair' to the landlord is in terms of the landlord as a capitalist investor, compared to investors in other markets, while 'fairness' to the tenant is understood in terms of every household's right to shelter, to the declared policy aim of successive governments of a decent home for everyone at a price they can afford (Department of Environment 1971, para 5; Department of Environment 1977a, para 2.16). The needs of an individual landlord and tenant may happen to coincide, either temporarily or for a long period, but there is no reason to believe that there is some formula which could transcend this innate conflict for the sector as a whole.

Moreover, where the landlord-tenant relationship is in conflict, then the 'personal' nature of this relationship, far from being an advantage, becomes a disadvantage to the tenant, who is inhibited from pursuing his or her rights under the law. This is not just a question of the difficulty of a tenant enforcing statutory rights against a hostile or threatening landlord; it will also be difficult for a tenant to do so against a 'reasonable' or 'paternalistic' one, because of the personal and individual nature of the contract.

In the public sector the objective of the landlord is in principle quite different from that of the private landlord. It is to provide adequate accommodation without a profit motive and subject to the democratic control of the community. This accountability moreover can be extended to give tenants more direct control over the management of their accommodation and, at the limit, to enable them to set up housing co-operatives. Moves towards tenant control in the private sector on the other hand are essentially moves *away* from private renting towards either some form of social renting or owner-occupation. Renting from the public sector also avoids the problem of personal relationships. The impersonal and bureaucratic nature of public renting can then be seen as advantageous, in that it permits tenants both individually and collectively to enforce their rights against a *corporate* body which is held to be both democratically accountable to the local electorate as a whole, and as having in some sense a public duty to its tenants.

In principle there should be no difference in the cost of providing private and public sector accommodation in equilibrium. In the private sector the landlord would receive a normal rate of return on three elements: finance, management and risk-taking. The public sector would have to borrow the finance (unless it was raised directly from taxation, a policy which has never been pursued in the UK) and pay for the management. Finally, risk-taking for the same good, housing, could be expected to be similar, affecting the required rate of return equally. In practice there are two reasons to expect differences. On the one hand, the private landlord has a considerable incentive to minimise costs while in the public sector it is often argued that the incentive for management is to make life easy for themselves and in particular to have a cosy relationship with employees, construction firms and the Housing Committee. This might lead to higher unit costs in the public sector (indeed, it is a major reason given for privatisation in housing [Whitehead, 1984]). On the other hand, the risk premium is in practice likely to be far higher in the private sector than in the public. This is partly because of the lack of confidence in the sector arising from the continuing political conflicts about how it should operate, but also because it is generally accepted that the public sector can borrow at lower rates as the government implicitly provides a guarantee against losses. It is possible that owner-occupation has lower costs for many types of household and dwelling in this respect than either rented sector, and this is a significant cause of the large proportion of housing in that sector. On direct cost alone it is likely that the social sector can at least be made cheaper, even if at the present time there are very significant inefficiencies. However, the importance of the two types of cost will vary between different household types and contractual relationships and private renting can be expected to be cheaper for at least some groups.

When there is disequilibrium in the housing market and demand exceeds supply, many of the benefits of private renting for the tenant are likely to disappear. In particular the benefits of choice and flexibility and the capacity to move house fairly frequently, which some authors argue gave tenants more equal power with landlords during the period when private renting was the mass tenure (e.g. Ward 1985, pp. 36–38) are no longer available. In these circumstances landlords are likely both to discriminate against certain groups which they perceive as likely to increase their costs of renting, and also to increase rents above the level necessary to provide an adequate return on capital. In these circumstances private renting will become unsuitable for a higher proportion of households – those without market power. However, in periods and areas of excess demand, it is also likely to be extremely difficult to gain access to local authority housing especially for non-family households. Some lower income households are then likely to have little or no choice other than to enter the private rented sector. Thus, paradoxically, as private renting becomes less desirable the numbers constrained to enter it may even increase.

Even in times and places where there is no shortage of accommodation low incomes are likely to mean that many households are unable to afford socially adequate accommodation without subsidy towards their housing costs. If such subsidy is inadequate the private rented sector may again be the only source of accommodation, owner-occupation being excluded because of the household's lack of resources and public renting because of inadequate supply. But what will be provided will be what the market is prepared to supply: low quality, overcrowded accommodation which allows the landlord some return on capital. In these circumstances, tenants gain few if any of the benefits of flexibility and choice which might be expected to flow from private renting.

Thus where capacity to pay is low or demand outstrips supply private renting is likely to be an important source of accommodation – but little of that supply is likely to meet the requirement of a decent home at a price that the household can afford.

The picture that we have set out describes a two-stage process. First, there are inherent differences between tenures, both between owner-occupation and renting and between different forms of renting which means that households are likely to prefer different tenures because they rank these attributes differently. The attributes that differentiate owner-occupation and renting

141

relate to the separation of asset ownership and consumption; renting providing lower transaction costs and generally easier access, less responsibility for upkeep of the asset and less need to commit resources to ownership of the dwelling. These must be weighed against the problems of the landlord-tenant contractual relationship inherent in separation.

Factors that differentiate private from social renting relate to the different reasons for provision by private and social landlords, differences in the relationship between tenants and their landlord, different forms of monitoring and different levels of accountability. Generally one can expect the private relationship to be more flexible and the incentives for efficient provision to be greater. On the other hand, social landlords can be expected to take account of need rather than demand and to ensure that their accommodation meets socially defined standards.

In an ideal world one would expect tenure choice to reflect the different preferences for these attributes together with any differences in the cost of provision. Such costs would arise mainly from differences (a) in the costs of organising the landlord-tenant contract as compared to joint ownership and consumption; (b) in the costs of management and maintenance; and (c) in the risk involved in financing the asset. There are reasons to expect owner-occupation to be relatively cost-effective under the majority of circumstances with respect to the first two elements: (i) because it replaces the contractual relationship and because joint ownership and occupation may result in less wear and tear; and (ii) through the use of leisure time to maintain the property (Whitehead 1984). Where households have limited resources risks could be higher in owner-occupation while social renting might be expected to attract a lower risk premium if only on grounds of diversity. Such differences in cost may modify the household's choice of tenure, especially when they do not have strong preferences. The optimal mix of tenures will thus be determined both by tastes and by differences in the resource costs of provision reflected in the relative prices faced by consumers.

Second, these choices will be affected by differences in prices and constraints on choices which do not reflect differences in real resource costs. These factors in reality are for many households likely to be far more relevant than underlying preferences and resource costs because the housing system is so heavily distorted. There are four main areas of distortion which tend to lead households to favour owner-occupation as compared with renting and social renting as compared with private:

(i) *Present and past subsidy policies*: It is accepted by virtually all commentators that private renting has received minimal levels of subsidy in comparison to the two main tenures (Grey et al. 1981; Ermisch 1984). In recent years this government has particularly favoured owner-occupation, with comparatively little general subsidy going into either of the rental tenures (National Federation of Housing Associations, 1985b). The result is that private renting offers particularly poor value for money for occupants, who consequently will feel inclined to look elsewhere for their housing even where the attributes of private renting may be more desirable to them than those of either public renting or owning.

(ii) *Restricted availability of rented homes in both sectors*: Demand for rented homes has generally exceeded supply, for a variety of reasons which include the incentives in the general subsidy system, the constraints on private landlords through the effects of the Rent Acts, the financial caution of many local authorities, and latterly the effects of central government control over public expenditure resulting in a fall in new public sector building at the same time as a reduction in the existing stock through the sale of council houses (Forrest and Murie 1984b). For those able to obtain public sector housing, landlord-tenant relationships are likely to be better than those in the private sector where landlords have often wielded significant market power. The

143

limited range of dwelling types and location even when rented property is available further distorts choice towards owner-occupation.

(iii)*Imperfections in the finance market and particularly the effects of inflation in the 1970s*: These have meant that most households could not borrow significantly for any reason other than to purchase owner-occupied dwellings. Borrowing is particularly desirable during periods of low or negative real interest rates as experienced in the 1970s. The incentive to become an owner-occupier for investment reasons has therefore been very great.

(iv)*Ideological and social pressures*: Both political parties have spoken of the aspiration to home-ownership as a 'basic' or 'natural' desire (Gray 1982b). This has been compounded since 1979 by a government committed to the idea of privatisation, resulting in an increase in the stigmatisation of renting particularly in the public sector.

Who will and should the sector serve?

The effect of these distortions has been to shift both preferences and choices away from renting in general, and private renting in particular, towards owner-occupation. As we have already pointed out in Chapter 4, the evidence is that under current conditions this process is by no means complete. The size of the private rented sector can be expected to dwindle even further as traditional tenants die, move in with relatives or move to e.g. public sector sheltered accommodation, and are only partially replaced by a different type of tenant, who either has particularly strong preferences for the attributes of private renting that we have described or is unable to gain access to the majority tenures. Furthermore, as we have also seen in Chapter 4, the sector in the 1990s is likely to be dominated by non-manual rather than manual groups; geographically by agricultural and growth regions such as East Anglia and the South-West rather than declining regions

144

such as the North-West and the West and East Midlands; and in terms of household type by single people and other sorts of childless households, with very few family households remaining.

Given the scenario, we can identify the following sources of continuing demand within the current system:

(i)   *Lettings in relation to employment or business*: While the demand from some occupational groups, e.g. farm workers, is likely to decline as the number of jobs in these areas is reduced, demand from others, such as police and the armed services, will probably remain fairly constant. There could also be an increase in employment-related accommodation being offered by firms in the South East in order to attract certain types of skilled labour from other parts of the country. Such additional accommodation is likely to be temporary.

(ii) *In coastal and some rural areas* there will be a continuing demand from retired people, those seeking second homes and those wanting genuine holiday lettings.

(iii) *Luxury up-market lettings*, mostly in London, for international business people, diplomats, etc. As London becomes more and more a focus for European and international rather than domestic capital, demand from this group is likely to increase. Estate agents active in this market report continued growth in demand (Mitchell 1985).

(iv) *Moving owner-occupiers who require temporary accommodation*: As more households become owners, and a higher proportion of building society advances are given to moving owners rather than first-time buyers, it seems likely that more and more households will want private rented accommodation while they sort out their next owner-occupied dwelling. This is particularly relevant in a period of restructuring in the labour market. This

145

tendency could be partially offset if restrictive practices by exchange professionals are reduced and 'one-stop' property shops prove successful, but the problems of long-distance moving and choice will remain.

(v) *Households forming for the first time*: The extent of demand from this group will depend on changes in access to the two main tenures. Demand here is likely to come from a range of income groups, but may be increasingly dominated by non-manual groups who have greater market power. There is evidence linking new households who enter the private rented sector with later owner-occupation, while new households who start off sharing or concealed within another household are more likely to go on to become public sector tenants (Madge and Brown 1981, p. 155; Forrest and Kemeny 1982). These housing market linkages are likely to strengthen.

(vi) One particularly relevant subset of new households is that composed of *students*. There is unlikely to be much increase in owner-occupation among this group, and hard-pressed local authorities are unlikely to give them much priority for council housing (though some councils have found them a suitable group for otherwise "hard to let" property). However, their importance may lessen in the 1990s as the numbers of people in the relevant age group decline.

(vii) *Other, usually unmarried, younger households who wish to move fairly frequently,* either for housing or more likely for job reasons. Here again, this demand group is likely to be increasingly composed of professional and non-manual workers who may actively prefer renting to owning at the early stages of the life-cycle when several geographical moves may be necessary for career purposes.

(viii) *Households formed as a result of divorce or marital separation*: Such households will generally require only interim accommodation, while awaiting legal proceedings in relation to the marital home, the release of equity or the result of application to the local authority for housing. Others will remarry or form new consensual unions. Present trends in relation to marital separation and divorce suggest continuing demand from this group.

All these groups are likely to have positive preferences for certain aspects of private renting, mainly relating to flexibility and the capacity to change one's housing decisions with little cost. They are thus the types of household for whom policy makers are likely to take the view that private renting is an acceptable, or even desirable, option. Even among these groups there may be some households for whom it is not desirable – for instance lower income newly forming or moving family households, and similar households who have just suffered from divorce or separation. Such households would normally be expected to be better housed in the social sector. At best, private renting may be suitable temporary accommodation for these households.

In addition to these groups there will also be for many years to come a continuing demand from:

(ix) *The rump of traditional households who are already living in the sector*: Such households do not generally wish to move even though they are often living in poor quality accommodation. Where their circumstances do change, e.g. because of increasing age or disability, social renting is likely to prove a more suitable form of tenure.

(x) Similarly, except for particular types of retirement accommodation (listed under (ii) above) one would expect that *potential tenants looking for long-term secure accommodation and for limited responsibility with respect to repairs and maintenance* would generally find social renting more suitable. Only if such accommodation were unavailable would one expect to find any significant demand for private renting from this source. Such demand would be undesirable in policy terms.

In addition, there may be forced demand arising from:

(xi) *Evictions from the public sector and families deemed 'intentionally' homeless*: Although families are likely to become increasingly rare in the PRS, and the Homeless Persons Act should ensure that the public sector is the 'tenure of last resort' for families, there will still be some who are excluded from the public sector and forced into the private rented market.

(xii) *Other low income households, particularly the single,* but including other non-traditional households who cannot afford owner-occupation and are unable to gain access to public sector accommodation. The importance of this group is likely to vary significantly between areas, being concentrated in London and other areas of high prices and general excess demand. This demand will continue to come both from those who prefer to rent, and from those with little or no other alternative.

Sources of supply

The types of accommodation required by these groups are extremely heterogeneous, ranging from the very high quality, high-amenity properties in the luxury sector to that demanded by students where, above a basic minimum, low cost and convenient location are likely to be given higher preference than amenity, and to job-related demand which is likely to be similar to mainstream family demand in the majority tenures with an added locational component. The price people are willing and able to pay also varies greatly among these different groups, with some households able to pay a very high price for convenience and quality while others are totally dependent on the welfare system. Supply to meet this demand depends upon a range of factors, including (a) the commercial viability of expected rental income as compared to other opportunities available to potential landlords; (b) the effectiveness of security of tenure and other restrictions on forcing existing landlords who would like to leave the sector to remain; (c) the extent of non-commerical provision by private individuals, and (d) the benefits to employers of providing accommodation for their employees.

The main sources under (a) are likely to be types of letting where either the return for one reason or another does not relate to the full capital value of the property or the capital value itself is particularly low. Additionally, in areas of high demand for particular types of property some lets covering full market value will be feasible. Under (a) are included:

(i)   lettings by *resident landlords*, i.e. owner-occupiers letting part of their own home in order to obtain a contribution towards the owner's mortgage and other expenses. It is difficult to gauge the exact size of this sub-sector as a considerable part of this activity probably takes place in the 'black economy', with owners not declaring the income for tax or other reasons. It has often been suggested that the growth of owner-occupation, especially among lower income and elderly households, would increase the supply of such accommodation. However, as described above (see p. 54), there is no evidence of any absolute increase in the size of this sub-sector although it may be growing in relative terms (Paley 1978; Todd et al. 1982; Todd 1986).

(ii) *temporary lettings provided by owner-occupiers* while the owner is abroad, working elsewhere in the UK etc. These lettings are likely to increase, given generally higher levels of owner-occupation, the geographical restructuring of job opportunities and growing internationalisation of at least some sectors of the labour market. Such landlords are likely to be prepared to let as long as the rent covers the costs of letting and the risk of problems arising from poor upkeep or obtaining repossession.

(iii) *temporary lettings of property bought as a retirement or second home*: This source may also increase with rising levels of owner-occupation and second-home ownership, although its viability will depend on housing remaining a good investment in comparison to other possibilities available to the individual.

(iv) *property physically unsuited for sale to owner-occupiers*: This may be because of remote location, or because the property is only partly residential, e.g. flats above shops, or because unusual design or construction makes it unmortgageable, or because of particularly poor physical attributes or condition.

(v) *property in areas of generally low demand*, especially at the bottom end of the housing market where the filtering process has resulted in very poorly maintained unsuitable units. Such dwellings will have a low value in the owner-occupied market, and the return available on letting to households dependent on housing benefit and with few other opportunities may therefore be greater (Crook and Bryant 1982; Martin 1983; Martin 1985). A guarantee of income provided by the benefit system sets a minimum value for tenanted property which can be higher than that provided by demand for owner-occupation. It is not likely, however, to be high enough to make it worthwhile for landlords to make any additional investment, e.g. in improvement, except where substantial grants are available.

(vi) *temporary lettings of property where landlords can obtain improvement grants*. Even where the landlord's eventual aim is sale into owner-occupation, the conditions attached to improvement grants mean that the property must be let for a minimum of 5 years (Martin 1983, 1985).

(vii) *dwellings in multiple occupation* let at high densities which enable landlords to obtain a large rent stream, often for low quality accommodation with shared amenities. Such lettings are likely to be viable in areas of high demand, especially where the property is difficult to convert into units suitable for owner-occupation.

(viii) *up-market, centrally located properties bought for investment purposes,* mainly in London, by absentee (often foreign) owners, and let in the interim (Mitchell 1985).

(ix) *other lettings suitable for employed non-traditional households,* especially young professionals, where turnover can be expected to be rapid and there are thus few restrictions on sale into owner-occupation as and when required by the landlord. Sources of supply here might include inherited property while the beneficiaries decide what to do, as well as those who expect capital values in housing to continue to rise and therefore regard it as a good quality flexible investment if desirable types of tenant are available.

Under (b) are included:

(x) *lettings with full security of tenure*: Many landlords (possibly still the majority) cannot obtain possession of their properties until the tenant or his/her successor volunteers to leave. Such landlords are obliged to continue letting or to sell to others who are prepared to do so. It is extremely unlikely that any future government would extend deregulation to the majority of these tenancies, as a large proportion of the tenants are pensioners and most have been living in the accommodation for many years. However, a large

151

proportion of landlords would not continue to let on the same terms once the opportunity to recover possession arises. It seems reasonable to assume that, given the age structure of the tenants, such opportunities are likely to arise for the majority of such landlords over the next decade or so. When it does, the decision to relet will depend upon similar factors to those listed under (i) – (ix).

(xi)   Some re-letting may occur when possession is obtained because *only part of the property becomes vacant*. Such lettings will normally be less secure than the original lettings, enabling the landlord to sell up when the rest of the property becomes vacant (Whitehead 1978).

(xii) *lettings made in the belief that they were outside the Rent Acts* which turn out to be secure. Changes in the interpretation of the law on e.g. licences, company lets and shorthold tenancies may result in a small number of such properties remaining in the sector even when the landlord wishes to withdraw. Given the way that the Rent Acts have operated over the last decade and the low proportion of new lets which are perceived by landlords and tenants to be covered by the Acts (House of Commons Environment Committee 1982a, 1982c; Pearce 1982; Greater London Council 1985, 1986), the size of the sub-sector which is constrained to remain is likely to fall significantly over the next decade – to be replaced if at all by lettings which are commercially viable.

Under (c) there is an unknown but significant number of owners letting for altruistic, family, charitable and other non-commercial reasons. Why such lets occur has not been studied in detail so it is difficult to predict the future size of the sector. The sorts of factors which might affect it are on the one hand a growing desire on the part on the elderly to live separately (many such lets in the past have probably been to elderly relatives) and the apparently inexorable growth in demand for privacy, both of which will tend to reduce supply; and on the other hand the growing number of households which are inheriting property at a time when they are already well-housed and who may be prepared to let to friends and relatives rather than sell; and the growth in co-operatives and other intermediate tenures which may include communal provision for unrelated people on non-commercial terms.

Finally, under (d), employers may continue to let when the job requires the employee to live near the work or actually on the premises. There may also be some provision by employers who find it desirable to offer accommodation in order to attract staff. High house prices in areas of recent rapid economic growth, such as the M4 corridor, have led to complaints from employers about the difficulty of recruiting suitably skilled labour. If this continues, employers may find it desirable to intervene in the housing market by providing accommodation directly to some of their employees. However, the majority of such assistance will probably be in the form of loans to assist employees to buy their own homes.

These fourteen categories probably represent the main sources of continuing supply of privately rented accommodation in the medium term. They suggest that the majority of such supply will come from existing poor quality units with a small number of luxury lettings for professional households that want to rent. Significant new build or improvement investment for private rental both seem extremely unlikely under current conditions, although there are reports of some evidence of the latter outside London (Martin 1983, 1985). The government has on several occasions promoted the idea of building societies and other financial institutions providing rental units at market rents (e.g. the 'assured tenancy' scheme introduced by the 1980 Housing Act), but unless considerable subsidy were attached it seems un-likely that this could provide a viable rate of return. At the present time it seems most likely to occur, if it occurs at all, in the social sector via the financing of housing associations.

153

If there were to be an increase in demand there seems no reason in principle why supply should not be forthcoming to provide for those with the capacity to pay. The two main factors stopping any such expansion are the lack of purchasing power of the majority of those who are looking for accommodation in the private rented sector, which makes it unprofitable to provide reasonable quality accommodation, and lack of confidence on the part of landlords about the terms and conditions under which they will be legally enabled to let. In the final part of this paper we discuss the basic policy choices available given this scenario.

1. We do not, of course, mean by this that the expansion of owner-occupation has meant the end of conflict in the housing market. Potentialities for conflict exist between outright owners and mortgagors, between owners as a whole and exchange professionals, between different sorts of owner-occupiers, and between owners and tenants.

Chapter 6   Policy implications and conclusions

Introduction

The picture presented in Chapter 5 suggests that there is a basic dichotomy with respect to demand which policymakers must take into account when determining how to organise the private rented sector in the future. On the one hand there are a significant number of households that would prefer private rented accommodation mainly for short periods. Such households have reasonable market power and should therefore be able to make a suitable contract with the landlord, unless there is a shortage of accommodation. On the other hand there are existing and potential tenants who have very limited power because they cannot readily obtain accommodation elsewhere and have little puchasing power in the rented market. Such households are not normally in a position, unaided, to make an effective contract with a private landlord. Nor does the landlord have any incentive to provide adequate accommodation because what the tenant can pay is below the cost of provision of minimum standard housing. This situation is made far worse in areas (such as London) where there is an overall shortage of accommodation so that market rents are far above the cost of provision.

On the supply side a similar distinction can be made between landlords who are happy to provide accommodation (not necessarily on terms which are desirable) under current conditions and those landlords who remain in the sector against their will. In the long run, landlords cannot be forced to provide accommodation and to invest in the sector. Rent control and security of tenure do enable tenants to remain in their homes against the landlords' wishes but once that tenant (or the successor) leaves, the landlord can make a free decision as to what to do with the property. In the meantime, the lack of choice on the part of the landlord has costs: he is unlikely freely to undertake repair, maintenance and improvement expenditure or to uphold the contract with the tenant in an acceptible fashion. Enforcement of controls and standards is certain to be both costly and incomplete in these circumstances.

What therefore is desirable in the longer term is a situation where landlords and tenants are all volunteers (i.e. landlords wish to let given the alternative investments available to them and tenants want to rent privately); where there is a reasonable choice of accommodation available to all types of tenants so that tenants are able to make a contract on equal terms with the landlord; where there are alternative forms of tenure available for those for whom private renting is not suitable; and where tenants and potential tenants have the capacity to pay for at least minimum standard accommodation. Such a scenario is unlikely to result in a sector which was larger than at present. Indeed, almost certainly it would be smaller, because the attributes of private renting are not desirable for the vast majority of households, although the optimum size depends as much on what was happening in other tenures as in the private rented sector itself. Ideally, the size would reflect both private choice and any social benefits such as those related to flexibility in the labour market.

The problems involved in reaching this ideal position are exacerbated by the difficulty of setting up suitable transitional arrangements – given the large number of long-term tenants who live in secure accommodation where the landlords are dissatisfied with conditions. A pre-condition for any proposed reform must be that these tenants, often elderly and nearly always poor, must be fully protected by any policy initiative.

The current position is, however, clearly undesirable on almost

157

all possible grounds. Although rent control and security legislation does succeed in providing secure accommodation for a significant number of tenants, many of these have to live in quite inadequate physical conditions – and the numbers helped by the legislation continue to decline rapidly. On the other hand, the effect of the legislation, together with the availability to landlords of investment opportunities elsewhere, is to reduce the supply of accommodation to new and potential tenants. For those with the capacity to pay for owner-occupation or to enter the public sector, this simply reduces choice and forces people to make long-term and expensive commitments at times when this is not desirable. For those with few other alternatives to private renting, the results may often be appalling: poor quality and value for money for those who do find something in the sector, while for those who do not, either highly insecure and unsuitable 'non-tenure' accommodation, or having to remain living with other people. Moreover, the law is brought into disrepute because it is seen as being incapable of dealing with problems of avoidance and evasion, even though the vast majority of tenants and landlords are able to come to some sort of agreement.

Even among this group there are a large number of tenants and landlords who are disadvantaged by the lack of certainty about the nature of their agreements, especially whether they are covered by the Rent Acts. This uncertainty both reduces the landlords' incentives to supply and often means that tenants are frightened of enforcing the terms of their agreements for fear of losing their accommodation.

The choices available

In examining what can be done in order to improve the situation, it is necessary to specify the conditions in which such changes might be implemented. For instance, a policy such as allowing the market to set rents might be desirable where there was neutrality of subsidy between tenures and a balance between demand and supply area by area. However, these are not feasible conditions at the present time. We therefore limit most of our discussion to a situation where supply conditions vary between areas, where public provision of rented housing is unlikely to increase significantly in the short term and where owner-occupation remains relatively favoured in subsidy terms.

Under these conditions there are a number of possible policies that could be introduced with the aim of improving conditions in the sector, most of which would help some groups at the expense of others. The choice of policy therefore dependes upon value judgements about the likely effectiveness of each measure and the relative weights given to gainers and losers.

The main forms which policy changes can take are reasonably well understood. They relate to

(i) the legal framework in which lettings take place, and

(ii) the taxation and subsidy system as it applies to landlords and tenants.

With respect to (i), the possibilities range from completely removing controls over rent and security to tightening up these controls and applying them to all forms of letting. With respect to (ii), possibilities that are usually discussed include increasing assistance to tenants, improving the taxation position of landlords and subsidising some types of (or in the extreme, all) private landlords who provide adequate accommodation.

The most important groups who are likely to be differentially affected by changes in the legislative system are existing and potential private tenants and existing landlords and those prepared to put investment into the sector. With respect to (ii), additional resources for private renting must come from somewhere, either from reductions in other housing subsidies or from general taxation or cutbacks in public expenditure elsewhere.

Here we examine the two main approaches to legislative change – reducing and increasing controls – and in each case ask what

159

these imply for taxation and subsidy policy if the private sector is to operate effectively.

An effective market

In trying to assess what can be done it is important to distinguish between those problems that arise from shortage and those that would occur even if there was accommodation readily available at a price which covered the opportunity cost to the landlord. In a situation where the number of potential tenants is roughly equal to the supply of rented housing, significant problems would still remain. These are the problems experienced in large parts of the country outside London, the South East and some conurbations: basically those of low quality, inadequate choice in terms of price and type, and unsuitable contractual arrangements.

The problems of contractual arrangements are inherent in the landlord/tenant relationship and the specificity of individual tenancies (see Chapter 5 above). It can be argued that, in areas where there is generally adequate supply, these problems may be reduced by a basically two-fold approach, as follows:

(i) as is the case in several European countries (Harloe 1985), legislating for a standard contract which would operate wherever a better contract was not negotiated and which would cover minimum rights of occupation, tenure and payment, perhaps including a modified version of the conditions of the 1954 Landlord and Tenant Act which applies to commercial property. This would allow market rents but also give the tenant first refusal at the end of each contract under well-specified conditions;

(ii) setting up an arbitration system within this legal framework to deal with problems which arise between individual landlords and tenants – in other words, recognising that the landlord/tenant relationship is a personal one certain to produce highly differentiated problems which cannot be effectively dealt with by general legislation. This problem has been recognised in the labour market, where the employer/employee relationship is similarly individual, and arbitration procedures have existed for many years. Proposals for a Housing Court have been put forward regularly over the last decade – including detailed suggestions from the Law Society. Also, there is plenty of experience to draw on from abroad, notably New York where such courts operate cheaply, without undue formality and at times when tenants and landlords can appear without difficulty (Harloe 1985).

Changes of this type would simplify the legislative framework significantly – in itself highly desirable   but would remove security of tenure and rent control for new tenancies. They would however clarify the position of both landlord and tenant and this certainty would be desirable. It should provide an incentive for landlords who are currently marginally unprepared to let to enter the market. However it would, in principle, reduce the rights of some 80% of new tenants who are currently covered by the Rent Acts. Whether or not this group would perceive themselves as being worse off depends upon a set of trade-offs between a better structure for private agreements (which is the way that most of these tenancies operate anyway), and the lack of recourse to the legal framework of security and control when things go wrong and between potentially higher rents and the possibility of easier access to accommodation.

Certainly some tenants would be worse off: both those who have successful recourse to law under the current legislation and the much larger group whose landlords take the current law into account when making private agreements – perhaps not forcing rents up to what the market might bear or accepting that the tenant has long-term security even when this is not fully spelled out. On the other hand, there should be easier recourse to an arbitration system and greater certainty should anyway reduce the need for such recourse. Further, if the conditions of the 1954 Act were included, these would specify how renegotiation of contracts at the end of each term would operate, and provide long-term security at market rents for tenants who kept their tenancy conditions and wanted to remain.

Whether or not rents would be higher and access easier depends upon the supply response to the freedom to set rents and conditions. In some parts of the country there is evidence that market rents in the unfurnished sector are similar to or even below the fair rents set by Rent Officers (House of Commons 1982a, para 42). The supply is of poor quality older units that have low values in the owner-occupied sector and where, while the return on current values may be adequate to ensure letting, the incentive on the part of landlords to put any additional capital into the accommodation is minimal. It seems likely that in a freer market additional supply of accommodation would be forthcoming but that it would mainly be of similar quality and type. Such housing would not be suitable for long-term tenants and indeed not always adequate for many of those looking for shorter-term lets.

This relates to the second major problem which would occur even in a market without shortage: the limited capacity to pay of the majority of tenants. If the market were much freer one could expect a growth in demand from higher income tenants who did not want to incur the high transaction costs of owner-occupation. This demand should induce a supply of suitable accommodation, but the size of the sub-sector would remain limited by the better opportunities available to households in the owner-occupied market. Expectations of continuing capital appreciation in the owner-occupied market would reduce it further. Within the current subsidy framework the majority of tenants would continue to be those with few alternatives, mainly because they cannot gain access to tenures more suitable for their needs. If it remains true that their capacity to pay is too low to provide an acceptable return on capital to the landlord, only property with few if any alternative uses will remain in the sector and repairs and maintenance will continue to be skimped.

There are three possible approaches to this problem: reducing the costs of provision of adequate accommodation; increasing the incomes of those confined to the sector so that they can afford a rent acceptable to the landlord; or directly controlling the price. The first is infeasible – the cost of new investment in housing is certain to remain above the affordable level for many households. Without intervention households will be forced into low quality accommodation which is running down towards dereliction or into living at unacceptably high densities, often sharing facilities. The third, price controls, has been tried and has failed because it reduces the landlords' incentive to supply. Giving a subsidy to landlords to cover the difference between the rent payable by the tenant and that required by the landlord is almost certainly politically unacceptable in the private sector (but see below, pp. 165 –6). This leaves an income supplement – e.g. the extension of housing benefit to all households so that they can afford reasonable accommodation – as the best available possibility.

The difficulties with this approach are threefold. First, take-up is almost inherently limited where the assistance has to be specifically requested from a third party (unlike, for example, local authority tenants who are already in contact with the relevant agency). However, it is in the interests of landlords to ensure that their rent, and an adequate rent, is paid; this problem may be partially overcome by targetting information etc. on landlords as well as tenants. If the tenancy includes reasonable contractual conditions and there is little tax liability, the disincentives for landlords to be involved, obvious at the present time, would be less, although there will always be some who are not prepared to be involved with bureaucracy.

Second, housing and household circumstances change more often in the private rented sector, making it difficult to keep up with the complex adminstration currently involved in operating housing benefit. The scheme must necessarily be simplified if it is to be effective at the margins of the housing system.

Third, if the majority of households are dependent upon assitance and the majority of capital involved has little value elsewhere, the market may not set rents effectively. Instead, rents may be pushed up without any increase in quality. This can only be solved by ensuring both an adequate supply of accommodation so that there is a choice available to tenants and some incentive for tenants to exercise economy – e.g. by relating housing benefit to area rents rather than those of the individual property (National Federation of Housing Associations 1985b; Whitehead and Kleinman 1986). It would also be desirable for rent to be made dependent upon adequate repair and maintenance standards. A version of this approach has been used with some success in the United States in the Section 8 programme (Harloe 1985). There is also a significant problem of public expenditure arising from higher benefits and take-up as well as the possibility that assistance would be open-ended because it would induce additional household formation. Again this requires careful specification of the scheme in relation to social objectives; but the general need for additional subsidy arises from the inadequacy of current assistance to the sector.

Such assistance is absolutely necessary if those at the bottom end of the market are to be enabled to obtain reasonable housing. It will require the transfer of resources from other parts of the economy. These can probably best be obtained from a reallocation of subsidies to owner-occupation, although under current conditions such a transfer seems highly unlikely (National Federation of Housing Associations, 1985b). More fundamentally, differences in relative power would remain between the landlord and tenant, even where the availability of housing benefit improved the tenant's spending power. Such a system entails the provision of considerable sums of public money to private landlords with, in practice, comparatively little control over quality of accommodation and standards of management. Moreover, this financial assistance would be channelled through low-income households who are probably the most market-weak of all groups, through lack of information, lack of resources and social or economic disadvantage. In many ways this would be uncomfortably close to the present situation in regard to board and lodging arrangements, which combines large payments to private landlords from the public purse (DHSS in regard to single people, local authorities in regard to homeless families in bed-and-breakfast) with absence of consumer choice and often very poor standards both of accommodation and management (Conway and Kemp 1985). Before the problem can be avoided, tenants and potential tenants must have a real choice between tenancies and moreover be aware of that choice. Even in areas where there is little pressure this position is unlikely to be achieved.

Lastly, any change which increased the range of options open to a landlord who can gain vacant possession of a currently protected letting must produce some increment in the incentive to obtain such possession via harassment, winkling, or moral pressure exercised against currently protected tenants. To the extent that transfer to other tenures remains the favoured option for such landlords, this effect will be limited and restricted to property types which are not readily saleable into owner-occupation. The group it would mainly affect would be those who live in property which could be more profitably used differently within the sector – e.g. through sub-division and higher density of occupation or by transfer to the short-term market. While in principle additional safeguards could be brought in to protect such people, the difference in relative power of landlord and tenant, the age and poverty of many of the tenants concerned, and the inadequate record of public agencies in tackling harassment, suggest scepticism about the efficacy of any such additional protection.

Another possible approach is to direct subsidy to supply so that market rents are reduced to more affordable levels. The political objections to subsidising private landlords are very strong and have so far proved overwhelming. However, there might be some possibility of classifying certain types of landlords (such as financial institutions) who would be eligible for subsidy under

165

strict conditions with respect to management, maintenance and access. This is one of the main suggestions of the Inquiry into British Housing (National Federation of Housing Associations 1985b) and there has been considerable interest in such proposals, particularly from building societies. This would extend the range of tenures, filling a gap left by the demise of the large private landlord interested mainly in rental income. At the limit such landlords would resemble housing associations fairly closely. Another possibility would be to provide subsidy while rents were held at fair rent levels but to allow market rents without subsidy after some period.

The obvious alternative remains that those without adequate income should transfer to the majority tenures where a better level, and take-up, of assistance is available. Given current restrictions on supply in the social rented sector, this perhaps seems an unlikely scenario. Yet it would seem rational to ask those who wish to rely on the private sector on what grounds they regard private landlords as more effective than public, especially for long-term provision for lower-income households.

Problems of shortage

The scenario that we have so far examined applies only when demand and supply are in rough equilibrium. It is inapplicable in areas of shortage, notably London where there is a very different ratio between existing secure tenants and those with limited protection or unable to gain access. For instance, in London the furnished sub-sector accounts for about 40% of private lettings as compared with about one-quarter elsewhere, and the growth of 'non-tenure' accommodation is almost wholly concentrated in London and a few other urban stress areas. There is thus a very different trade-off in these areas: can removing controls ensure enough additional supply to provide adequate accommodation for those now excluded from the sector, as well as give reasonable choice to tenants and keep rents to normal profit levels?

Under current conditions this seems highly unlikely. The GLC survey and other evidence suggest that rents in the regulated part of the sector are in many cases as low as one third or even one quarter of what they would be under free market conditions (Greater London Council 1985, 1986; House of Commons Environment Committee 1982c). It also suggests that the return on capital, even at these higher rates, is often inadequate to keep the property in the sector. Only certain resident landlords, up-market company lets and some dwellings in multiple occupation where density of occupation is high, clearly yield returns which make commercial letting worthwhile. Freeing up the market would thus be likely both to raise rents significantly and to reduce total supply of existing units.

Would these higher rents bring in a new type of supply? To the extent that the majority of new lettings (which are mainly furnished, converted accommodation) are made formally or informally outside the Rent Acts and yet the supply of new lettings continues to decline, the answer would seem to be no (Whitehead 1983a, 1985a). Rents on these lettings are mainly already set by what the market will bear – and this is inadequate to ensure a steady supply at prices potential tenants can afford. The result is that many are excluded from the market altogether while others have to accept poor standards, lack of privacy and sometimes overcrowding.

Were there to be all-party agreement about removing controls (which is unlikely in the extreme), the effect might be to increase supply somewhat through a reduction in uncertainty about the future. The supply elasticity with respect to such a change is unknown, although the effects of the 1957 Act suggest that probably the overall effect would still be counter-productive, at least in the short run. In the longer term, the existence of profitable opportunities may offset this effect – but the period involved is likely to be politically too long and too stressful, perhaps resulting in the re-imposition of controls and a further disincentive to let.

With decontrol there would be some additional incentive for landlords with secure tenants to try to obtain vacant possession – because the return in the newly-freed market would be higher. There is no reason, however, to think that it would change their incentive to obtain possession to transfer the property to other tenures. While a return to the extreme forms of 'Rachmanism' prevalent after 1957 seems unlikely, there would be increased pressure on some tenants, ranging from financial incentives to outright harassment. Strong guarantees for such tenants would be a prerequisite of any legislative change, but even with these, the problem is likely to remain, for the reasons stated above.

The main question remains: will there be a strong enough incentive for landlords to continue to let vacant units and to bring additional units on to the market? And if there is, do these benefits outweigh the costs of increased uncertainty to secure tenants and the inequity of large lump-sum capital gains to landlords who generally bought at tenanted prices?

Only if the existence of adequate returns in the sector is obvious can landlords be expected to accept the opportunities made available to them by any legislative changes. The most effective way of ensuring these returns is to enable tenants to pay prices equal to opportunity cost rents. If this could be done via improved housing benefit, the effect then depends on there being an adequate existing supply of accommodation which can rapidly be brought into private renting. As these units have left the sector but have not usually disappeared altogether, additional supply could in principle become available reasonably rapidly. But such a reversal in behaviour would be highly unlikely unless both investment opportunities were reduced elsewhere (e.g. by the reduction of subsidies to owner-occupation) and faith in the sector were restored. These conditions will almost certainly not obtain. Instead it is far more likely that supply adjustment would be slow, the effect of decontrol would then be to raise rents for at least that part of the sector where rents are affected by the existence of controls and few would be any better off. The case for decontrol is thus more complex in areas of shortage. On the one hand, the potential incentive to provide accommodation is clearly far higher than in areas of balance and the benefits of such additional provision are similarly higher. But so are the costs, because those who are currently protected receive very significant benefits. The stakes are therefore very much higher and to make decontrol a reasonable choice in this context, the potential for a significant supply response would have to be demonstrated. Paradoxically, therefore, the case for decontrol is probably weaker in areas of shortage than elsewhere.

Additional controls

The alternative put forward by those who stress improving conditions for existing tenants is to legislate to enforce controls more effectively and to extend these controls to all parts of the sector.

In areas of adequate provision the effects would probably be fairly limited. Those who already have secure tenancies would be in the same position as at present – and therefore better off than under any version of decontrol which could not provide absolute guarantees to all now covered. Among those who have tenancies under private agreements the level of perceived security might be greater, but otherwise there should be little difference because demand is anyway roughly equal to supply. However, there might be an adverse effect on new supply in the long term because of the lower possibility of obtaining repossession when desired. This will reduce incentives to let for potential landlords, particularly those who wish to enter the market for short periods for personal reasons.

Where the immediate problems would arise would be at the margins of the sector where, even in areas of generally excess supply, there are likely to be conditions that are worse than would be legally allowed. Here there would be an increased incentive for landlords to leave the sector as soon as the property became vacant. The extent of this effect of course depends upon the alternatives available. However, experience of response to past changes suggest it could be expected to be quite significant, at least in the short run. In other words, at the worst if the new legislation were effective, one could expect to lose most new lettings which are now made at rents above fair rents, or with conditions less than those intended by the Rent Acts. The less effective the legislation, the less would be this loss. But the problems of uncertainty and insecurity on the part of both landlord and tenant then remain.

In areas of shortage one could expect the effect to be very much worse, because alternative investments are more likely to be available. The effect of fully comprehensive legislation would be to help those who are currently insecure – a not insignificant number, perhaps as many as one third of all private tenants in London. However, by no means all these actively benefit from security because a proportion would anyway expect to move on fairly rapidly. In London, for instance, 20% of tenants had moved in the last year at the time of the 1983 GLC survey, although, in an unknown number of these cases, the causality would have been in the opposite direction, i.e. mobility resulted from insecurity of tenure (Greater London Council 1986). More importantly, new lettings would certainly be reduced significantly because market rents are generally so far above fair rents. Again, the 1983 GLC survey suggests that market rents in London are at least 70% higher than fair rents for similar property (Greater London Council 1986). The effect of this would be to push even more people into 'non-tenure' accommodation or simply to stop them forming separate households at all.

This suggests that while there would be benefits from increasing controls for a proportion, possibly a large proportion, of existing tenants, these are likely to be offset by the costs to potential entrants who would find far less accommodation available, especially in areas of shortage.

Some of these adverse effects could be alleviated by

accompanying increased controls with respect to security with higher rent levels. At the limit this would be equivalent to a modified assured tenancy scheme relating to existing property with market rents but long-term security.

The worst of all possible worlds would occur if, while attempting to tighten up the legislation, it proved impossible to make the new controls effective. Under these circumstances, landlords' confidence in the sector would be reduced and supply would therefore fall, conditions at the margin would worsen yet existing tenants would not obtain the benefit of greater certainty about their position.

What should be done?

Neither extending nor removing controls therefore seems likely to solve the current problems, especially in areas of shortage. Perhaps the best that can be achieved in the short run is to tidy up the legislation in order to clarify the position of both existing landlords and tenants and to introduce a comprehensive list of Rent Act exclusions which refer to those situations where statutory control is neither necessary nor desirable. Other contractual arrangements would be regarded as inside the Rent Acts. This would reduce uncertainty for both landlord and tenant.

Yet the basic fact remains that landlords cannot be expected to continue to provide accommodation under reasonable conditions unless they receive a return commensurate with that available elsewhere and that at the present time this is not the case. Increasing controls or making them stick more effectively will always reduce supply in the long run. This would be an acceptable cost if:

– there were a large number of existing tenants who would benefit, and

– there were better alternatives available to potential tenants.

Neither of these conditions are now met. On the one hand

longer term tenants are generally covered by the Rent Acts and would gain little from their extension. On the other, perhaps the most important conclusion of our analysis of the current position of the sector is that 'non-tenure' accommodation, which provides even worse conditions and value for money than the private rented sector, is now growing rapidly as the private rented sector continues to decline. Controlling the sector further, without improving access (particularly for new households) into either owner-occupation or the social rented sector, would be likely simply to force more people into non-tenure accommodation.

Further, only if additional accommodation can be made available for poorer households who have little market power can the underlying problems of shortage in many areas be eased. We see little chance of this occurring in the normal private rented sector because there is so little incentive for landlords to provide adequate accommodation except at the upper end of the market, where short-term accommodation for those in employment can be profitable. Even in areas where there is no overall housing shortage the quality that the majority of tenants can afford is very low. Tenants and potential tenants everywhere need more help to achieve acceptable standards and in some areas there must be additional investment.

It therefore seems inescapable that the declared policy goals of successive governments of a decent home for every household at a price they can afford cannot be achieved without the provision of additional rented accommodation and that this in the main can best come from the social housing agencies: local authorities and housing associations.

The alternative of inducing supply by private landlords via large-scale payments through the housing benefit system can only be justified if there is reason to believe that the private sector can better meet the requirements of households in that tenure. In Chapter 5 we suggested that there are good reasons to expect the public sector to be more effective than the private at providing finance more cheaply, and bearing the risks of renting. However, we also suggested that the private sector may have more incentive to manage efficiently. This suggests that in the longer run there is a case for building up more mixed tenures where public and private sectors both have a role. The purely private sector would be restricted to providing low risk, high management accommodation – basically shorter-term lets to those with reasonable ability to pay. For those households who need greater security and help towards their housing costs and who would perhaps benefit from a more socially aware management, the proportion of public sector involvement should increase. In other cases provision would be wholly by the public sector, because the costs of less cost-conscious management would be more than offset by the benefits of a lack of a market incentive to exploit the tenant who has little or no market power.

Such a scenario is based on there being a neutral tax and subsidy system in which households can choose between tenures on the basis of their suitability to their personal requirements, and on a level of subsidy which enables all to afford reasonable quality. It cannot be achieved without large-scale supply adjustment in areas of shortage, much of which could however take place within the existing stock.

The private rented sector can have a significant and desirable part to play in the adjustment process, if political agreement about its long-term role can be achieved. But there is every reason to believe that for the majority of those looking for long-term secure accommodation private renting as currently understood can never be suitable. The aim of policy should therefore be not the revival, in numerical terms, of the private rented sector, but rather a realignment by which those who want its desirable attributes are enabled to find suitable housing in the sector and those for whom it is inherently unsuitable are readily housed elsewhere.

To arrive at this desirable state of affairs would require policymakers to accept that the private rented sector does have a long-term role in the British housing system, but one that is likely to be small in absolute terms, and to relate mostly to younger middle- and higher-income households. Its potential for adequately meeting the housing needs of those looking for longer-term tenancies and for tackling the acute problems which remain in many urban areas appears to be minimal. In particular, the access crisis in London and elsewhere requires an immediate and sustained increase in the provision of good quality rented housing, for both family and non-family households. The benefits of achieving this by making greater resources available to a range of socially orientated rental agencies, rather than through the private rented sector, seem obvious, however unlikely such a solution appears at the present time.

Bibliography

ATKINSON, A.B. and KING, M.A. (1980) 'Housing policy, taxation and reform', *Midland Bank Review*, Spring, pp. 7–15.

AUDIT COMMISSION (1986) *Managing the Crisis in Council Housing*, HMSO, London.

AUSTERBERRY, H., SCHOTT, K. and WATSON, S, (1984) *Homeless in London*, I.C.E.R.D., London.

AUSTRALIAN BUREAU OF STATISTICS (1983) *Census of Population and Housing, 30 June 1981: Summary Characteristics of Persons and Dwellings, Australia*, C.J. Thompson, Commonwealth Government Printer, Canberra.

BALCHIN, P. (1985) *Housing Policy: An Introduction*, Croom Helm, Beckenham.

BANK OF ENGLAND (1982) 'Mortgage lending and the housing market', *Bank of England Quarterly Bulletin*, Vol. 22, No. 3, pp. 390–398.

BODDY, M. (1980) *The Building Societies*, MacMillan Press, London.

BUILDING SOCIETIES ASSOCIATION (1983) *Housing Tenure*, B.S.A., London.

BURNETT, J. (1978) *A Social History of Housing 1815–1970*, David & Charles, Newton Abbott.

CONWAY, J. and KEMP, P. (1985) *Bed and Breakfast: Slum Housing of the Eighties*, SHAC, London.

COOPER, S. (1985) *Public Housing and Private Property*, Gower, Aldershot.

CROOK, A.D.H. and BRYANT, C.L. (1982) *Local Authorities and Private Landlords: A Case Study*, Sheffield Centre of Environmental Research, Sheffield.

CROOK, A.D.H. and MARTIN, G.J. (1986) Decline and Change, Investment and Disinvestment: Patterns of Change in Private Rented Housing in Inner Sheffield since 1979, Paper given at the Rowntree Conference on Private Renting at the University of York, July.

DEPARTMENT OF ENVIRONMENT (1971) *Fair Deal for Housing*, Cmnd 4728, HMSO, London.

DEPARTMENT OF ENVIRONMENT (1977a) *Housing Policy, A Consultative Document*, Cmnd 6851, HMSO, London.

DEPARTMENT OF ENVIRONMENT (1977b) *Housing Policy Technical Volume, Part I*, HMSO, London.

DEPARTMENT OF ENVIRONMENT (1977c) *Housing Policy Technical Volume, Part II*, HMSO, London.

DEPARTMENT OF ENVIRONMENT (1977d) *Housing Policy Technical Volume, Part III*, HMSO, London.

DEPARTMENT OF ENVIRONMENT (1979) *National Dwelling and Housing Survey*, HMSO, London.

DEPARTMENT OF ENVIRONMENT (1982) *English House Condition Survey 1981, Part 1*, HMSO, London.

DEPARTMENT OF ENVIRONMENT (1983a) *English House Condition Survey 1981, Part 2*, HMSO, London.

DEPARTMENT OF ENVIRONMENT (1983b) *Third Report of the Advisory Committee on Rent Rebates and Allowances*, HMSO, London.

DEPARTMENT OF ENVIRONMENT (1983c) *Housing and Construction Statistics 1972–82*, HMSO, London.

DEPARTMENT OF ENVIRONMENT (1985a) *1981 Based Estimates of Numbers of Households 1981–2001*, HMSO, London.

DEPARTMENT OF ENVIRONMENT (1985b) *Beacons Exercise: Feedback for 1 January 1985 Return*, mimeo.

DEPARTMENT OF ENVIRONMENT (1985c) *Housing and*

Construction Statistics 1974–84, HMSO, London.

DEPARTMENT OF HEALTH AND SOCIAL SECURITY (1986) *Reform of Social Security – Programme for Action*, Cmnd 9691, HMSO, London.

DOLING, J. and DAVIES, M. (1984) *Public Control of Privately Rented Housing*, Gower, Aldershot.

ENGLISH, J. (1982) (ed.) *The Future of Council Housing*, Croom Helm, London.

ERMISCH, J. (1984) *Housing Finance: Who Gains?*, Policy Studies Institute, London.

EVANS, A.W. (1985) *Urban Economics*, Blackwell, Oxford.

FORREST, R. and KEMENY, J. (1982) 'Middle-class housing careers: the relationship between furnished renting and home ownership', *Sociological Review*, Vol. 30, No. 2, pp. 208–221.

FORREST, R. and MURIE, A. (1984a) *Right to buy? Issues of need, equity and polarisation in the sale of council houses*, Working Paper No. 39, School of Advanced Urban Studies, University of Bristol.

FORREST, R. and MURIE, A. (1984b) *Monitoring the right to buy 1980–1982*, Working Paper No. 40, School of Advanced Urban Studies, University of Bristol.

GAULDIE, E. (1974) *Cruel Habitations: A History of Working-Class Housing 1780–1918*, Allen & Unwin, London.

GRAY, F. (1979) *Consumption: Council house management*, Chapter 8 in Merrett (1979).

GRAY, F. (1982a) *The exchange process*, Chapter 13 in Merrett (1982).

GRAY, F. (1982b) *Owner-occupation and social relations*, Chapter 15 in Merrett (1982).

GREATER LONDON COUNCIL (1985) *'Going...going... almost gone': Preliminary Report on a GLC Survey of Private Tenants in London 1983–84*, GLC, London.

GREATER LONDON COUNCIL (1986) *Private Tenants in London: The GLC Survey 1983–84*, GLC, London.

GREY, A., HEPWORTH, N. and ODLING-SMEE, J. (1981)

Housing Rents, Costs and Subsidies: A Discussion Document, 2nd revised edition, CIPFA, London.

HARLOE, M. (1985) *Private Rented Housing in the United States and Europe*, Croom Helm, Beckenham.

HOLLAND, M. (1965) *Report of the Committee on Housing in Greater London*, Cmnd 2605, HMSO, London.

HOUSE OF COMMONS ENVIRONMENT COMMITTEE (1982a) *The Private Rented Housing Sector, Volume I, Report*, HMSO, London.

HOUSE OF COMMONS ENVIRONMENT COMMITTEE (1982b) *The Private Rented Housing Sector, Volume II, Minutes of Evidence*, HMSO, London.

HOUSE OF COMMONS ENVIRONMENT COMMITTEE (1982c) *The Private Rented Housing Sector, Volume III, Appendices*, HMSO, London.

HUGHES, D. (1981) *Public Sector Housing Law*, Butterworth & Co., London.

HUGHES, G.A. (1979) 'Housing income and subsidies', *Fiscal Studies*, Vol. 1, No. 1, pp. 20–38.

HUGHES, G.A. and McCORMICK, B. (1981) Do council housing policies reduce migration between regions? *Economic Journal*, Vol. 91, pp. 919–937.

KARN, V., KEMENY, J. and WILLIAMS, P. (1985) *Home Ownership in the Inner City: Salvation or Despair?* Gower, Aldershot.

KEMP, P. and RAYNSFORD, N. (1984) *Housing Benefit: The Evidence*, Housing Centre Trust, London.

KLEINMAN, M. (1984) 'Private rented sector remains poor relation', *Housing*, August, pp. 19–22.

KLEINMAN, M., PEARCE, B. and WHITEHEAD, C. (1985) 'Housing: twenty-five popular fallacies', Department of Land Economy Discussion Paper No. 14, University of Cambridge.

LANSLEY, S. (1979) *Housing and Public Policy*, Croom Helm, London.

LEGRAND, J. and ROBINSON, R. (1984) *Privatisation and the*

Welfare State, Allen & Unwin, London.

MACLENNAN, D. (1982) *Housing Economics*, Longman, Harlow.

MADGE, J. and BROWN, C. (1981) *First Homes: A Survey of the Housing Circumstances of Young Married Couples*, Policy Studies Institute, London.

MALPASS, P. and MURIE, A. (1982) *Housing Policy and Practice*, MacMillan Press, London.

MARTIN, G. (1983) *Landlord Improvement Activity since 1980*, Occasional Paper TRP 43, Department of Town and Regional Planning, University of Sheffield.

MARTIN, G. (1985) *Rebuilding the Private Rented Sector: Interviews with Improving Landlords*, Department of Town and Regional Planning, University of Sheffield.

McGURK, P. and RAYNSFORD, N. (1984) *A Guide to Housing Benefits*, Institute of Housing/SHAC, London.

MERRETT, S. (1979) *State Housing in Britain*, Routledge & Kegan Paul, London.

MERRETT, S. (1982) *Owner Occupation in Britain*, Routledge & Kegan Paul, London.

MITCHELL, V. (1985) 'Too hot to handle', *Savills Magazine*, No. 11, pp. 11–17.

NATIONAL FEDERATION OF HOUSING ASSOCI-ATIONS (1985a) *Inquiry into British Housing: The Evidence*, NFHA, London.

NATIONAL FEDERATION OF HOUSING ASSOCI ATIONS (1985b) *Inquiry into British Housing: Report*, NFHA, London.

NEVITT, A.A. (1966) *Housing, Taxation and Subsidies*, Thomas Nelson & Sons, London.

O.P.C.S. (1982) *Labour Force Survey 1981*, HMSO, London.

O.P.C.S. (1983a) *General Household Survey 1981*, HMSO, London.

O.P.C.S. (1983b) *Recently Moving Households: A Follow-up to the 1978 National Dwelling and Housing Survey*, HMSO, London.

O.P.C.S. (1983c) *Census 1981 National Migration Great Britain Part 1*, HMSO, London.
O.P.C.S. (1983d) *Census 1981 Housing and Households England and Wales*, HMSO, London.
O.P.C.S. (1983e) *Census 1981 National Report Great Britain Part 1*, HMSO, London.
O.P.C.S. (1984) *General Household Survey 1982*, HMSO, London.
PALEY, B. (1978) *Attitudes to Letting in 1976*, HMSO, London.
PEARCE, B.J. (1982) 'The Rent Acts 1968 and 1974: aspects of avoidance and evasion', unpublished Ph.D thesis, Department of Land Economy, University of Cambridge.
RAUTA, I. (1986) *Who would prefer Separate Accommodation?* HMSO, London.
ROBINSON, R. and O'SULLIVAN, T. (1983) 'Housing tenure polarisation: some empirical evidence', *Housing Review*, Vol. 32, pp. 116–117.
SPENCE, M. (1975) *Market Signalling*, Harvard University Press, Harvard.
TODD, J., BONE, M. and NOBLE, I. (1982) *The Privately Rented Sector in 1978*, HMSO, London.
TODD, J.E. (1986) *Recent Private Lettings 1982–84*, HMSO, London.
UNITED STATES, BUREAU OF THE CENSUS (1983) *The 1980 Census*, USGSO, Washington DC.
WARD, C. (1985) *When We Build Again*, Pluto Press, London.
WHITEHEAD, C.M.E. (1978) 'Private landlords in London: who stays, who goes?', *CES Review*, No. 4, pp. 48–52.
WHITEHEAD, C.M.E. (1980) 'Fiscal aspects of housing', in C. Sandford, C. Pond and R. Walker *Taxation and Social Policy*, Heinemann, London.
WHITEHEAD, C.M.E. (1983a) 'Can private renting survive?', *Estates Gazette*, 21 May, pp. 691–693.
WHITEHEAD, C.M.E. (1983b) 'Housing under the Conservatives: a policy assessment', *Public Money*, Vol. 3, No. 1, pp. 15–21.

WHITEHEAD, C.M.E. (1984) 'Privatisation and housing', in Legrand and Robinson, 1984.

WHITEHEAD, C.M.E. (1985) 'Government guarantees needed to rebuild private rented sector', *Building Societies Gazette*, July, pp. 832–835.

WHITEHEAD, C.M.E. and KLEINMAN, M. (1985) 'The private rented sector: a characteristics approach', *Urban Studies*, Vol. 22, pp. 507–520.

WHITEHEAD, C.M.E. and KLEINMAN, M. (1986) 'Capital Value Rents', Paper given at the Rowntree Conference on Private Renting at the University of York, July.